POWer of Worship
POWer of the Word
Creative Children's Church Curriculum

Wherefore seeing we also are compassed about with so great a cloud of witnesses, let us lay aside every weight and the sin which doth so easily beset us, and let us run with patience the race that is set before us.
Hebrews 12:1

Word Aflame Publications
PENTECOSTAL PUBLISHING HOUSE
8855 Dunn Road   Hazelwood, MO 63042-2299
Printed in U.S.A.

Editor . . . . .R. M. Davis
Associate Editor . . . . .P. D. Buford
Children's Editor . . . . .Barbara Westberg
Editorial Assistants . . . . .Becky Christman
                                                    Linda Gunn
                                                  Karen Myers
                                                  Joni Owens

Editor in Chief—UPCI . . . . .J. L. Hall

✎ Writers
Janice Roberts
Brenda Soptelean
Paula Townsley
Barbara Westberg

✂ Layout
Joni Owens

☞ Art
Georgia Smelser
Elizabeth Swisher

❏ Cover Photographer
Classic Portraits by Wayne

☆ On Cover
Scott Jenkins
Amber Martin
Ryan Anderson

🎓 Cover Art
Elizabeth Swisher

CURRICULUM COMMITTEE
James E. Boatman,
P. D. Buford,
R. M. Davis,
J. L. Hall,
G. W. Hassebrock,
Garth E. Hatheway,
E. E. Jolley,
E. J. McClintock,
Chester L. Mitchell,
W. C. Parkey,
David L. Reynolds,
Charles A. Rutter,
Berl Stevenson,
R. L. Wyser.

© 1996 by
Pentecostal Publishing House,
Hazelwood, MO 63042
All rights reserved
ISBN 156722041X
Permission to copy scripts and art
granted for local church use only.

Word Aflame Staff

True Winners 4
kids POWer hour Staff 5
An Overview of *kids POWer hour* 5
Junior Olympics 6
The Winner's Series, LaMarque, Texas 8
Unit I Introduction 9
Unit II Introduction 32
Unit III Introduction 65
POWer hours 10-96
POWer house papers 97-122
Art 123-127
Songs 128

UNIT I A Winning Team—Jesus and Me 9
1. **My Best Friend** (Mary, Martha, and Lazarus) 10
2. **My Shepherd** (David Keeps the Sheep) 16
3. **My Healer** (The Woman with an Infirmity) 21
4. **My Savior** (The Samaritan Woman Meets the Savior) 26

UNIT II In Training 32
5. **I Am Gifted** (Miriam, Leader of the Rhythm Band) 33
6. **I Can Develop My Gifts** (David, Sling Shot Champion) 40
7. **I Can Witness** (Naaman's Maid, a POWerful Witness) 47
8. **I Can Serve** (Elisha, a Prophet's Shadow) 52
9. **I Can Do My Best** (Moses, a Tongue-Tied Leader) 59

UNIT III Go for the Gold 65
10. **Hurdling Rejection** (Joseph Keeps a Right Attitude) 68
11. **Conquering Peer Pressure** (Daniel and the Hebrew Children Take a Stand) . .76
12. **Tackling Fear** (Esther Saves Her People) 82
13. **Defeating Inferiority** (Gideon Wins the Battle) 90

Permission is granted by Word Aflame Publications for the *POWer house* papers and the art in the back of this manual to be copied for local church use.

True Winners

What is a winner?

In a playground fight, the bully stands over a whimpering boy and raises his fist. His gang cheers. Is this kid a winner?

In a learning disability class a little girl struggles to arrange blocks in their proper sequence. She is the last one to finish, but she does finish. Is she a winner?

One can lose and still be a winner,
While one can win and still be a loser.

In our world winning is all-important to many. "Do whatever you have to do to win—just be sure you win," is their motto. Those who win at the expense of conscience, morals, and others lose far more than they gain.

The winner is not always the toughest, the first one to cross the line, or the one with the highest score.

The word "winner" is not in the Bible. Surprised? "Win" is only in God's Word twice and "won" three times. But the concept of winning is referred to many times. "He that overcometh. . .." (Revelation 2:7). "I have finished my course" (II Timothy 4:7). "This is the victory that overcometh the world" (I John 5:4).

One unusual definition of *win* is "to discover and open (a vein or deposit) in mining." Mining is hard, dangerous work. Often tons of dirt must be removed before a vein is discovered. Hours are spent working in the dark. Then when a strike is made, the profit goes to the company, not the miner. Sound like teaching?

Could it be that our children become winners when they "discover" their personal worth and "open" themselves to the probing work of the Spirit?

In every child is great potential; often it is hidden deep. In some their worth has been buried under an onslaught of verbal abuse. In others no one has taken the time to dig deep enough to uncover the talents.

Anyone who is teaching for personal recognition is sure to burn out quickly. But the teacher motivated by the love of God and children toils on—in the dark, removing tons of dirt—not sure what, if anything, he is accomplishing. He only knows that the potential for great value is there. Perhaps soon a strike will be made! If not, he has made it easier for the next teacher to make a strike.

In *The Winner's Series* we want to engrave in each child the knowledge that he has in him a vein or deposit of priceless value which is worth mining. We pray that the work of the Spirit will quicken the teacher's job. May each one leave *kids POWer hour* knowing that in Christ he is a winner—a true winner.

Barbara Westberg

A Winning Attitude

Help build a winner's attitude in your children—compliment the children by telling them they are winners, especially when they feel like they have failed. Use affirmative phrases often. "That's a winning attitude." "Great job." "You're tops." "Super." "Thanks for giving it your best shot."

kids POWer hour Staff

Director

In Units One and Two the director is referred to as the "coach." In Unit Three he is simply the "director." He leads the service and organizes activities. A good leader will delegate as much as possible.

Trainers

Teachers and assistants are "trainers" for *The Winner's Series*. Dressed in sweat shirts, tennis shoes, etc., each carries a whistle and a clipboard (a good place for a schedule and notes).

A music director and engineer are great helps. A trainer for each 6-8 children is a good ratio. However, many churches do not have this kind of help available. If you do not, do not despair. Use older children or younger teens for trainers. It will be good training for them and wonderful help for you.

Mascots

In Unit Two Professor N. A. Dither comes on the scene to add humor and interest to the lessons. In Unit Three two angels, Alpha and Beta, interact in skits and with the children to give an inside child-like view of the spiritual world.

An Overview of kids POWer hour

Units

Unit One, "A Winning Team," emphasizes the child's relationship with Jesus. During this unit, stress teamwork and utilize as many group activities as possible.

Unit Two, "In Training," reminds each child that he has great potential. It is designed to build the child's self-esteem and emphasizes that he "can do all things through Christ."

Unit Three, "Go for the Gold," shows the rewards which are ahead for overcomers. The children watch as Heaven's Heroes are crowned and march into eternal life to walk on gold. This unit deals with issues—rejection, peer pressure, fear, and opposition. People in the Bible faced and overcame these problems, just as children can do today.

Warm-Ups: Sing Unto the Lord

Theme songs for this quarter, along with puppet skits and some special messages from God's Word, are recorded on the *kids POWer hour* tape.

Each *kids POWer hour* make time for the children to present Dynamo Specials. This is the children's time to shine. They can sing songs, play musicals, recite verses of Scripture, read poems, show art work. As talked about in the editorial, "mine" for your children's talents and create ways they can perform.

Group introverted children with the extroverts. Be careful that a few outgoing children do not dominate this time. Give everyone a chance to shine.

Perfection is not the goal, participation is. Remind the children that they are not performing for personal glory, but to bring glory to God.

Knee Bends

One of the most important things we can teach children is how to pray.

Prayer time is an exciting time at *kids POWer hour*. Whatever physical position they take, children learn that prayer is a POWerful weapon God has given His children. A variety of activities, including a prayer spinner, are given to catch the children's interest and involve them in prayer.

Pushups

A variety of activities are interwoven into the testimony time. By testifying, children learn that lifting up Jesus in praise lifts them up in spirit.

Exercise: AIM

The Winner's Series is a good time to emphasize missions. The Olympics is an international sports event so "winners" from around the world can be recognized. Missionaries around the world are winners—winning souls for Jesus Christ.

Assign this portion of the hour to a trainer and call him or her the *POWer hour* AIMer (Associate in Missions). Each *POWer hour* the AIMer will give a report.

Decide on the countries and missionaries, preferably your church's Partners in Missions, to be featured in *kids POWer hour*. Missionary maps are included in the visual packets of Word Aflame Publications Sunday school curriculum each spring. Find one of these and display it in your children's church area. Designate your church's PIM's with a gold star. Connect your missionaries to their country with a gold cord.

Ask your pastor or missions director for PIM letters to share with the children. Look in an encyclopedia for each country's flag and other interesting information. Make simple flags and attach to small dowel rods. As each country is featured, hang its flag around the map.

If you do not have any or all of the missionary biographies published by Word Aflame Press, ask if there is anyone in your congregation who has these books and will loan them to you for this series. *Profiles of Pentecostal Missionaries*, compiled by Mary H. Wallace, is an excellent resource. These books should be read by the trainer chosen to be the AIMer. Also ask to borrow out-dated *Pentecostal Heralds* or *Global Outreaches*.

Mission Banks

Check with your pastor for permission to give your offerings in this series to missions. Ask for his suggestion for a special project.

On page 127 is a label which can be copied on colored paper (or colored by the children), and attached to a can.

You will need one empty, clean 14-16 ounce can for each child. Place a strip of duct tape around the rim to prevent cuts. Cans are open so the money collected can be removed for each *kids POWer hour*.

Encourage the children to take these "mission banks" home with them. Each *kids POWer hour* the children can give the money they have collected.

Make a graph so the offering can be charted. Children, as well as adults, give more when they know how much money is coming in and where it is going. Secrecy about finances tends to zip people's pocketbooks.

Do research on the monetary system of the country where your mission offering is going. Record the offerings in both your national currency and the foreign currency. The "cedis" (pronounced "c-d.'s) on the illustration is the currency used in Ghana, West Africa.

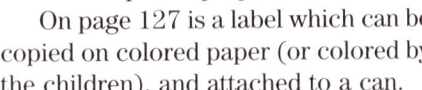

Junior Olympics

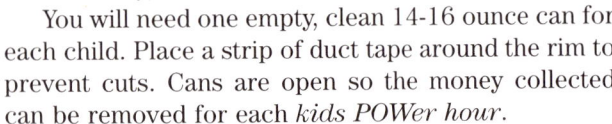

During or at the end of *The Winner's Series* have a Junior Olympics in the park (or if the weather is bad, in the fellowship hall or a gym).

As in all socials, organization is the key to success. Have a planning session with your staff. Divide into committees, *e.g.*, transportation, games, refreshments.

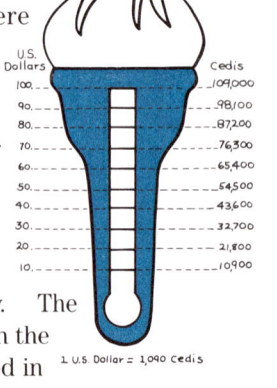

Plan on dividing the children into two groups—younger and older—for most games.

Plan an activity for each group for each 10-15 minute segment. The exception to this time limit could be a group game, such as, volleyball. Even in this case, there will be smaller children or those who do not like volleyball to entertain.

Remind the trainers that the Junior Olympics is a fun time for the children, not a time of fellowship for the adults. When the children are busy playing, chances for trouble are small. When they are bored, watch out! They will stray into forbidden areas, quarrel, and smaller ones may even fuss to go home.

Give each child a permission statement for the parents to sign. List time, location, and details of the outing. Also provide a place where a telephone number can be listed where the parents may be contacted in case of an emergency. A cellular phone number could be listed so the parents could contact their children, if a need arises.

Check with your trainers. What type of outdoor games are available? What is appropriate for the children's ages? Safety should be a major consideration.

Here are some game suggestions which require simple equipment.

Games

Since not all children are athletic, have a variety of games.

A Color Hit

Have the players count off by fours. Give each number a color, *e.g.*, one's can be red, two's blue, three's green, and four's yellow. After colors are assigned, choose one player to be "it."

Half of the children of each color stand on a line. The other half stand on a line about ten yards away.

"It" stands at either end of the lines, holding a soft, large ball. He calls out a color, "yellow." All yellows must change lines. "It" throws the ball, attempting to hit someone. If he succeeds, the one he hits becomes "it."

Water Balloons

Children love water balloon games. Use one of

these variations or make up your own.

(1) Divide into teams of six or so. Each team forms a circle and is given a water balloon. The team which keeps their balloon in the air the longest wins.

(2) Form two lines about 6' apart. Give a water balloon to the first player in line A and the last player in line B. The goal is to throw the balloon across the open space back and forth from player to player until it reaches the other end of the line. Since two balloons are going at the same time, this gets confusing and exciting. If a balloon touches the ground (and by some miracle does not burst), it is returned to the beginning of the line.

The losers are the ones who get drenched by a balloon when a balloon bursts. The game ends when both balloons burst or reach the end of the lines.

For variation, you may want to have several balloons ready and replace balloons as soon as they burst.

Bubble Gum Blowing Contest

Give each contestant a piece of bubble gum. Appoint two or three judges and see who can blow the biggest bubble.

A variation is to make each contestant stand with his hands behind his back and see who can blow six bubbles first. The catch to this is that fingers are usually needed to put the gum back in the mouth after a bubble has been blown.

Bubble Gum Relay

Divide into teams. Give each player a piece of bubble gum. At the signal, the first player on each team puts the gum in his mouth, chews, and blows a bubble until it bursts. After his bubble bursts, the second players puts his gum in his mouth, chews, and blows a bubble until it bursts. This is repeated down the line. Players must wait to put their gum in their mouth until the one ahead of them has burst his bubble. If a player breaks the rules, his team is eliminated. The first team to finish wins.

Indoor Tennis

Place a trash can on the floor. Three feet in front of it, place a chair with the back away from the trash can.

The player stands about 6' behind the chair. He tries to bounce a tennis ball so it hits the floor between him and the chair, goes over the chair, and into the trash can. Give each player five tries. If the ball goes into the can, but bounces out, the player gets fifty points. If it goes in and stays, he gets one hundred points.

Refreshments

Keep the refreshments simple. A menu of nachos or hot dogs, cookies, chips, and a soft drink is a hit with most children.

Finally

Gather the children around and have prayer before sending or taking them home.

Stick with the schedule. Even if everyone is having a wonderful time, get them home on time. It is better to end on a high note than drag it out until everyone is tired and fussy.

Learn from this experience. What worked well? What did not work? If there was a problem with a child, talk to your pastor and decide on the best course to take. It may need to be dealt with or simply ignored. Do not let one unruly child or one negative happening overshadow all the positive accomplished by this outing.

- -

An Overview of kids POWer hour

kids POWer hour is made up of two general parts: POWer of Worship and POWer of the Word.

To prepare for *kids POWer hour,* watch for these icons; they alert you to what is happening.

On Your Mark—a checklist of things to do before *kids POWer hour.* Some of these things may be done at home. Others are last-minute things to do in the room before the children enter.

The *Power Line* is the focus statement of the lesson. You will find it everywhere that message is repeated.

Praise Generators—songs, Dynamo specials, suggestions for prayer time, and testimony service ideas.

Truth Conductors—objects lessons, science demonstrations, illustrations, skits which transmit an important truth.

Energy Outlets—games, activities, projects which allow the children to move around and work off energy.

Plug Ins—teaching tips to plug the teacher into the lesson text, students' characteristics, what to expect, etc.

Spirit Generators—worship choruses designed to prepare the hearts of the children for the Word of God.

Life Transformers—the Illustrated Sermon which transforms children into spiritual dynamos.

Puppet Time—skits, announcements, songs which are written for (or can be adapted to) puppets.

The Winner's Series

Decorating can be so much fun! Here are some sample shots from Faith Tabernacle of LaMarque, Texas. Pastor Lynn Bohannon's wife, Teresa, and her "winning team" of workers have created a great *kids POWer hour*. Take note, use your imagination and the art included in the back of this manual, and be a **Winner for Jesus!**

Thank you, Sister Bohannon and Faith Tabernacle.

Additional photos on page 46.

Unit One
A Winning Team—Jesus and Me

TEAM WORK

Memory Passage: Hebrews 13:5-6

Unit Aim: To help children develop a personal relationship with Jesus Christ.

Theme Introduction

Passing the Torch

In 1928 the flame became a tradition for the Olympic games. The first torch relay was a twelve-day run to the Berlin games in 1936.

The flame for the Olympic games in Atlanta, Georgia in 1996 was lit in Olympia, Greece and arrived in Los Angeles in April. About 10,000 runners passed the flame along a route covering forty-two states and 15,000 miles. It traveled by steamboat, train, horseback, and wheelchair before arriving in Atlanta in July.

Construct an Olympic torch from stiff brown construction paper. Roll into a cone shape and secure with staples, glue or transparent tape. Stuff red tissue paper into the cone. Let some of the tissue paper fluff up to resemble "flames." Let this torch represent a signal for quiet. When the torch is held high, all should give their attention to the "torch-bearer."

The torch could also be used for testimonies or other activities. The leader gives the torch to one child who testifies, and then passes it along to another. Only the torch-bearer is allowed to speak.

Room Decor

Enlarge the art of the coach and the Dynamo kids running with the torch, doing knee bends and pushups. Make a large banner, *"The Winner's Series."* Hang it from the ceiling or mount it on the wall.

Enlarge the figure of Jesus from the back of this manual and place on the door or wall where the children enter the room. Directly across from this, place a full-length mirror. Above it display a sign, "A Winning Team: Jesus and Me." As each child enters the room, he/she will be able to look in the mirror and see both himself and Jesus reflected. This is a constant reminder that he is Jesus' teammate.

Place light exercise equipment, weights, etc., around the room. Let early arrivers use these (with supervision).

NOTE: The Memory Passage, Hebrews 13:5-6, actually begins in verse 5 with the phrase *"I will never leave thee, nor forsake thee."*

Just a Note

- In a three-ring binder keep a list of review questions, adding to it each week. This will be an instant source of questions for review games.
- Other items to add to this handy notebook:
  - Riddles and jokes which might be good for puppet plays.
  - Appealing decorating ideas.
  - Addresses, phone numbers, and birthdays.

Unit One   **A Winning Team—Jesus and Me**

Memory Passage: Hebrews 13:5-6

Unit Aim: To help children develop a personal relationship with Jesus Christ.

My Best Friend

Mary, Martha, and Lazarus

Scripture Text: Luke 10:38-42; John 11:1-12:8

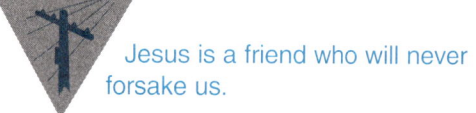

Jesus is a friend who will never forsake us.

Schedule

Date: _____

I. POWer of Worship (25-30 minutes)
  A. Coach's Clipboard (5 minutes)
    • Theme Introduction
    • Announcements
  B. Warm-ups (6 minutes)
    • Sing unto the Lord
  C. Exercise: AIM (6 minutes)
    • AIMer's Report
    • Special Mission Project
    • Mission Cheer
  D. Knee Bends (3 minutes)
    • Prayer/Praise Requests
  E. Pushups (3 minutes)
    • Testimony Time
  F. Dynamo Specials (5 minutes)
  G. Truth Conductor (8 minutes)
    • Friendship Punch
II. POWer of the Word (25-30 minutes)
  A. Training in the Word (5 minutes)
  B. Energy Outlet (5 minutes)
    • Concentration Game
  C. Biblical Calisthenics (5 minutes)
  D. Spirit Generator (2 minutes)
  E. Life Transformer (8 minutes)
    • Illustrated Sermon: Best Friends
  F. Invitation and Prayer (5-? minutes)
  G. Pass the Torch

 **On Your Mark**

✓ Study the feature pages and decide which activities you want to use.
✓ Schedule a meeting with the "trainers" (helpers), and delegate, delegate, delegate. Each trainer should bring (or be provided) a calendar to record his duties.
✓ Decorate.
✓ Make the Olympic torch as described on page 9. Or decide on another crowd control signal, such as, a whistle.
✓ Make flashcards for the mission cheer (under AIMer's report) and the memory passage, Hebrews 13:5-6.
✓ Make copies of the *POWer house* papers and mission can labels.
✓ Choose a country and missionary to be featured this *POWer hour*. Assign a trainer to do simple research and make the flag for your mission's display. If possible read a recent PIM letter from that country to the children. Make a paper or cloth flag of the country spotlighted for the wall missions display. See page 5 for ideas on ways missions can be emphasized in this series.

✓ Collect one empty, clean 14-16 ounce can for each child. Place a strip of duct tape around the rim to prevent cuts. Set up work tables for the mission banks. As children enter, direct them to a table where they color a label and glue it to a can. If everyone arrives at the same time (such as coming from Sunday school class), attach labels to cans beforehand. Children can pick them up as they leave.

✓ For the concentration game, you need twelve sheets of construction paper, the same color. Write "Mary" on two, "Martha" on two, "Lazarus" on two, "Jesus" on two, and leave four blank. Add simple shapes, *e.g.,* hearts, stars, triangles, for the non-readers. Use Plasti-Tak® to attach to the wall in a grid pattern, four across, three down, with the words facing the wall.

✓ Gather props for the Illustrated Sermon. Use trainers or older children (three boys and two girls) to pantomime the story. A practice is needed.

✓ Start a notebook as suggested on page 9.

Supplies

- ☐ *kids POWer hour* tape
- ☐ tape player
- ☐ review notebook
- ☐ clipboard
- ☐ brown construction paper
- ☐ staples, glue, or tape
- ☐ red tissue paper
- ☐ clean, empty 14-16 ounce cans, one per child
- ☐ duct tape
- ☐ mission can labels, one per child
- ☐ markers
- ☐ glue
- ☐ puppet
- ☐ flashcards of mission cheer and memory passage
- ☐ pitcher or punch bowl and ladle
- ☐ flavored drink powder
- ☐ sugar
- ☐ lemon-lime soda
- ☐ orange juice concentrate
- ☐ paper cups
- ☐ ice
- ☐ water
- ☐ construction paper
- ☐ Plasti-Tak®
- ☐ broom, rag, bucket
- ☐ copies of *POWer house* paper
- ☐ biblical costumes for Jesus, Lazarus, Mary, Martha
- ☐ apron, head scarf
- ☐ bed sheet
- ☐ ornamental box
- ☐ card table
- ☐ garbage bag

POWer of Worship

Coach's Clipboard (5 minutes)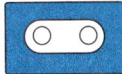

Introduce the theme by teaching children the song, "We Win, Hallelujah, We Win." Make announcements regarding special events planned during this series. Use the information on page 9 about the Olympic torch to acquaint children with the concept.

Warm-ups: Sing unto the Lord (6 minutes)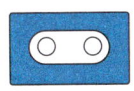

"If We All Pull Together"
"I'm in the Lord's Army"
"Jesus Loves Even Me"
"We Win, Hallelujah, We Win"
"He's Got the Whole World in His Hands" (Sing each child's name if time permits: "He's got Johnny Smith in His hands.")

Exercise: AIM (6 minutes)

Explain that an AIMer is an "associate in missions." Everyone who gives and prays for missions is an AIMer.

Call for the designated AIMer to give his or her mission report. Special emphasis should be placed on the sacrifice a missionary and his family make when they leave their home country to go to a foreign land. Discuss the loneliness missionaries endure when they do not know anyone and cannot speak the language. Point out that they have one Friend who goes with them everywhere. *Jesus is the Friend who will never forsake them.*

After a brief report, the puppet pops up and interacts with the AIMer to create excitement for the mission project. After announcing the details of the project, the puppet and AIMer use flashcards to teach the children this mission cheer (also on the *kids POWer hour* tape). Save the flashcards for future use.

AIMER: **Missions, missions is our theme.**
PUPPET/CHILDREN: **We're a mission-minded team.**
AIMER: **Missions, missions is our goal.**
PUPPET/CHILDREN: **Give to missions; win a soul.**
AIMER: **Can we do it?**
PUPPET: **Ab-so-lutely.**

CHILDREN: **Pos-i-tively.**
PUPPET: **Em-phat-ically.**
CHILDREN: **Un-mis-takably.**
PUPPET: **De-cid-edly—**
ALL: **Yes! M-I-S-S-I-O-N-S. Missions!**

Use the *kids POWer hour* tape to teach children the song, "Give and Pray." Let the children march around and drop their mission offering in a basket or special offering container.

Knee Bends: Prayer/Praise Requests (3 minutes)

Turn requests into praises! Instead of, "Jesus, please heal Erica's dad," pray, "Jesus, we thank You for healing Erica's dad!" Give thanks for the missionary families in the country studied today.

In keeping with "knee-bends," have the children kneel and raise their hands as they praise the Lord.

Maintain a victorious spirit—as becomes winners!

Pushups: Testimony Time (3 minutes)

Testifying in church is spiritual exercise, strengthening witnessing muscles.

Emphasize in testimony service that Jesus is the Friend who will never forsake us. Start by telling about a time when you were lonely or in danger and Jesus was with you. Pass the Olympic torch to a trainer and ask him to share a brief testimony also. These two testimonies should give the children examples to follow. As time permits, pass the torch to other children as they volunteer to testify.

Dynamo Specials (5 minutes)

Time for the children to develop their talents is important. Let them sing, recite verses, share art work, do charades, or play a musical instrument. Before calling on the children, emphasize that anything we do for God will be rewarded. God does not demand perfection, but participation. Make it plain that no one will be laughed at or put down.

POWer of the Word

Training in the Word (5 minutes)

All Olympians must train extensively to improve their potential for winning. Memorizing God's Word is part of our Christian training that makes us winners in life!

Divide the memory passage into three phrases and write them on flashcards. (Save the flashcards for future use.)

(1) *"I will never leave thee, nor forsake thee."*

(2) *"So that we may boldly say, The Lord is my helper."*

(3) *"And I will not fear what man shall do unto me"* (Hebrews 13:5-6).

Call a child to the front to perform a task such as moving the piano bench from one side of the room to another. When it becomes

---

Winner's Friendship Punch
(8 minutes)

Supplies for each half-gallon: 1 package of flavored drink powder, 3/4 cup sugar, 1 can lemon-lime soda, 1 small can of orange juice concentrate, and water to fill.

Mix the ingredients as you talk.

Friends can be found in all kinds of places—not just in church and school. Always be on the outlook for a new friend. Like these ingredients, individuals are lonely, but when we put them together in a friendly mix, we have something delightful. Let's call this drink Friendship Punch.

One way we serve Jesus is by serving our friends.

Choose volunteers to serve the punch. As the children enjoy the punch, encourage them to share friendship experiences, such as, "One time my best friend invited me to go fishing with his family." When possible, relate these experiences to our relationship with Jesus Christ.

Ask trainers to pass the garbage bag and collect the empty cups.

apparent that it is difficult to do the task alone, ask another child to help him. Discuss how teamwork makes the job easier.

Jesus is our teammate. He has promised that He will always be present to help us. Jesus is a friend who will never forsake us.

Repeat the memory passage one phrase at a time, using the flashcards. Then display them so everyone can see. Divide into teams and let the children help one another. Place older children with preschoolers.

Biblical Calisthenics (5 minutes)

We build our spiritual muscles by reading and memorizing God's Word. Let's do some biblical calisthenics.

Use this method to show the children how to find Luke 10:38. **Hold your closed Bible between your hands. With your thumb, open it in approximately the middle. It should open somewhere close to Psalms. Then hold the back half between your open palms. Again divide in half and open. It should open somewhere in the Gospels.** Instruct those whose Bibles opened to Matthew or Mark to turn to the right—as if they were continuing a story—to find Luke. Instruct those whose Bibles opened in John or Acts to turn back to find Luke.

The trainers should be ready to help anyone who needs it. Encourage children with Bibles to share with those who do not have one. Even preschoolers love to flip through the Bible and "read along."

This is a good time to teach the four Gospels. Most children are familiar with the game that calls out in rhythm, "Matthew, Mark, Luke and John." They may not be aware that these are the names of the first four books of the New Testament.

Repeat this exercise three or four times until the children can easily find Luke. Read Luke 10:38-42 dramatically as they follow along.

ILLUSTRATED SERMON

Best Friends (8 minutes)

Would you liked to have been in Mary and Martha's house that day when Jesus visited? Well, you can be—using that wonderful little device God planted in each of us—called "imagination." Pretend you are a little mouse in Martha's house. Be careful though and don't make a squeak because Martha is a super housekeeper. She will never allow mice in her house, if she can help it!

Scene I: Jesus Visits Mary and Martha

Present as a pantomime in a slow, thoughtful manner. Only the teacher speaks/reads. (The Scripture text, Luke 10:38-42, is from *New International Version*.) A practice session is necessary.

"As Jesus and his disciples were on their way . . ." Enter Jesus in white robe.

"He came to a village where a woman named Martha opened her home to him." Enter Martha wearing biblical robe, apron, and head scarf.

She carries a broom, rag, and bucket. Smiling, she opens the door for Jesus, motions Him to be seated, and then moves to the background.

"She had a sister called Mary . . ." Enter Mary in biblical robe.

Concentration (5 minutes)

Use this game to introduce the people in the Illustrated Sermon.

Instructions for making the grid for this game are under "On Your Mark."

Draw an invisible line down the center of the room, dividing into two teams. For a large group, choose two rows.

Teams take turns trying to find matching words by turning over two cards on the grid. The player should call out the words as he turns them over. If they do not match, he replaces them. If he has chosen a match, he keeps the cards for his team. The team with the most matches wins.

When all the cards are matched, ask if the children know the relationship between Jesus, Mary, Martha, and Lazarus. Answer: they were friends.

Lead the children in a worship chorus before the Illustrated Sermon. This quiets their spirits and prepares their hearts for the Word of the Lord.

"Who sat at the Lord's feet . . ." Mary sits on the floor at Jesus' feet.

"Listening to what He said." Mary gazes at Jesus with rapt attention.

"But Martha was distracted by all the preparations that had to be made." Martha moves to the front, looking agitated.

"She came to Him and asked, 'Lord, don't you care that my sister has left me to do the work by myself? Tell her to help me.'" Martha gestures frantically at Mary.

"'Martha, Martha,' the Lord answered . . ." Jesus looks tenderly at Martha.

"'You are worried and upset about many things, but only one thing is needed. Mary has chosen what is better, and it will not be taken away from her.'" Jesus gestures as He speaks.

As characters exit, discuss this scene with the children. **Who loved Jesus most, Mary or Martha?** Both loved Him. **Which sister did Jesus love the most?** He loved both the same. **What was most important to Martha?** Having a clean house for Jesus. **What was most important to Mary?** Visiting with Jesus. **Which was most important to Jesus, a clean house or a visit with His friend?** The visit.

Let's move on to another scene in the friendship of Mary, Martha, Lazarus, and Jesus.

Scene II: Lazarus' Death

Set up three chairs to form Lazarus' bed/grave. Lazarus enters and lays on the chairs. When he dies, Mary and Martha cover his face with a sheet. The "bed" becomes the "tomb." When he is resurrected, he gets up holding the sheet so that he appears bound in it. Detailed instructions are not given. As the teacher tells the story, the cast should act out their parts in the same manner as in Scene I. Optional: choose twelve children to be Jesus' disciples.

Lazarus was sick, terribly sick, and each day he grew worse. "If anyone can help Lazarus, it is Jesus," his sisters Mary and Martha decided. "We must send for Jesus right away."

It took the messenger two days to get to where Jesus was. "Your friend, Lazarus is very, very sick, Master. Mary and Martha need You to come immediately."

But strangely, Jesus did not seem concerned. He stayed two more days where He was. We know He loved Mary and Martha and Lazarus because the Bible plainly says so. But He did not run to help them.

Poor Mary and Martha. They were wringing their hands and crying. Where was Jesus? Why didn't He come when they called? They thought He was their friend.

After two days, Jesus said to His disciples, "Our friend Lazarus is dead. I am glad I was not there because something wonderful is going to happen which will help you to believe in Me."

By the time Jesus and His disciples arrived, Lazarus had been dead four days. Many of Mary and Martha's friends had gathered at their home to comfort them.

When she heard Jesus was coming, Martha ran out to meet Him. "Lord, if you had been here, my brother would not have died," she cried.

Jesus answered, "Your brother will live again."

Martha replied, "I know he will in the last day at the resurrection."

Jesus told her, "I am the resurrection and the life."

Then Martha sent for Mary. "Jesus is here and He wants to see you."

Mary came running. She fell down at His feet. "Lord, if You had been here, my brother would not have died."

Jesus asked, "Where is he?" They led Jesus and His disciples to the tomb.

When they saw Jesus crying, Mary and Martha's friends said, "Surely He loved Lazarus a lot."

"Take away the stone," Jesus ordered.

"Oh, Jesus," Martha gasped, "Lazarus has been dead four days. He stinks!"

Jesus looked at Martha. "Believe and you will see the glory of God."

So the people rolled away the stone and Jesus prayed. Then He called in a loud voice, "Lazarus, come forth."

Lazarus' body jerked to life. He got up and stumbled from the dark tomb.

"Loose him and let him go," Jesus ordered. With their mouths open in amazement, the people unwound the grave clothes from Lazarus.

Exit all.

Use these discussion questions to evaluate what the children learned from Scene II. **Why did Jesus wait two days before He started for Bethany to help His friends? How do you think Mary and Martha felt when Lazarus died and Jesus still had not come? Why was it better for Jesus to raise Lazarus from the dead than to heal him?**

Scene III: A Supper In Jesus' Honor

We find one more time just before Jesus was crucified when He visited with His friends, Mary, Martha, and Lazarus. We read about it in John 12.

Set up a card table. Jesus and Lazarus sit at the table. Martha serves them. Mary carries an ornamental box and pretends to anoint Jesus' feet as the teacher reads John 12:1-8, paraphrasing so the children understand.

Invitation and Prayer (5-? minutes)

Jesus was Mary, Martha, and Lazarus' best Friend. He wants to be your Best Friend, too.

Best friends spend time together. Right now we are spending time with Jesus in *kids POWer hour*. You talk to Jesus when you pray. You hear from Him when you read the Bible. You work with Him as a team when you witness, invite people to church, and serve others.

Have you heard of "fair weather friends"? These are friends who like you when everything is going right—when the weather is fair. But when you have trouble—stormy times—they disappear. Best friends are there for one another—in good times and in bad times. Jesus is a true Friend. He is a friend who will never forsake us.

When we have the Holy Ghost, it is the Spirit of Jesus living in us. This is how He is with us all the time. Quote together the memory passage.

Give children an opportunity to pray and seek the Holy Ghost.

Review Game

If there is time, play a review game, "Pass the Torch."

Remind the children to pick up their mission banks as they leave. Give each child a *POWer house* paper.

Review Game

Pass the Torch

Players divide into teams of two. They line up, with teammates holding hands. Give the Olympic torch to the youngest member of the first team in line. Ask them a review question. Teammates should confer before answering as they are allowed only one answer. If the answer is correct, they run around the room with the torch held high, holding hands. They run to the back of the line and give the torch to the team at the end. The torch is quickly passed up from team to team to the front of the line, and the process starts over. Any time a team misses a question or stops holding hands, they are out.

Unit One   **A Winning Team—Jesus and Me**

2

Memory Passage: Hebrews 13:5-6

Unit Aim: To help children develop a personal relationship with Jesus Christ.

My Shepherd

David Keeps the Sheep

Scripture Text: Psalm 23; John 10

The Good Shepherd provides for and protects His sheep.

Schedule

Date: _____

I. POWer of Worship (25-30 minutes)
   A. Coach's Clipboard (6 minutes)
      • Warm-Up Exercises
      • Brain Warm-Up Review Quiz
      • Announcements
   B. Warm-ups (8 minutes)
      • Puppet Sing-Along
      • Learn a Hymn
      • Dynamo Specials
   C. Exercise: AIM (5 minutes)
      • AIMer's Report
      • Mission Cheer and Offering
   D. Knee Bends (3 minutes)
      • Giving Praise Equal Time
   E. Pushups (3 minutes)
      • Testimony Time
   F. Pantomime (3 minutes)
      • "The Little Lost Lamb"
II. POWer of the Word (25-30 minutes)
   A. Training in the Word (5 minutes)
      • Reviewing Hebrews 13:5-6
      • Defining "Boldly"
   B. Biblical Calisthenics (5 minutes)
   C. Who Said That? (3 minutes)
   D. Spirit Generator (2 minutes)
   E. Illustrated Sermon (8 minutes)
      • David Keeps the Sheep
   F. The Shepherd Speaks (8 minutes)
   G. Prayer by and for the Pastor
   H. Wrap-Up: Bring Them In

 **On Your Mark**

✓ Decide on the country and missionary to be spotlighted by an AIMer. A flag of that country should be added to the display. Watch the *Pentecostal Herald* and *Global Outreach* for reports which could be used. In keeping with this *POWer hour's* material, emphasize the work of a missionary in finding the "lost." Be sure the children understand that the "lost" are people who have not obeyed the plan of salvation.

✓ Make four paper sack sheep puppets as instructed on page 17. These will be used by trainers and/or children for special singing. The same instructions are given on the *POWer house* papers so the children can make a puppet at home or, if time allows, at the end of *kids POWer hour.*

✓ Copy *POWer house* papers.

✓ Assign an older teen boy or man to play the role of David. It would be good if he can play a guitar. But, even if he cannot play, he carries one and strums on it occasionally as he talks. Give him a copy of the script so he can prepare. Ask him to come to *kids POWer hour* after the worship service has begun and sit among the children. If an extra man is not available for this role, when it is time for the Illustrated Sermon, the coach can simply put on a robe, pick up a guitar, and become David.

✓ For the game, "Who Said That?" record several people saying, "The Lord is my shepherd; I shall not want." Ask them to speak in a slow, clear tone. Leave a few seconds pause between each speaker. Be sure to include the pastor.

✓ Use the sheep pattern on page 126 to make a sheep for each child, plus a few extra ones. Use Plasti-Tak® or balls of masking tape to hide these around the room in fairly obvious places.

✓ Write on a board, flipchart, or transparency the first verse of "Amazing Grace." Create motions. Examples: "I once was lost"—place bowed head in folded arms. "But now I'm found"—raise arms in worship.

✓ Choose a small child to be "the little lost lamb" and an older child to be the shepherd. Make a sheep's head from a paper sack, according to instructions on page 18. Put this on the child. The "shepherd" wears a biblical robe and carries a "staff." As "The Little Lamb" on the *kids POWer hour* tape plays, the children pantomime it. Have a practice session.

✓ Tape a circle of colored paper underneath the seat of several chairs. The children in these chairs will be the ones who testify.

✓ If possible, arrange for the pastor (or one of his assistants) to come to the last half-hour of *kids POWer hour*. Ask him to be prepared to speak briefly to the children and answer any questions they may have about what it is like to be the "shepherd" of the church. Show him the schedule of the service so he can correlate what he says with the lesson plan.

✓ Cut name tags into the shape of lambs. As each child enters, write his name on one and put it on him.

✓ Add review questions to your notebook. Even if you do not think you will need them for this session, you will need them for review in another session.

Supplies

- ❏ *kids POWer hour* tape
- ❏ tape player
- ❏ *POWer house* papers
- ❏ name tags in the shape of lambs
- ❏ review notebook
- ❏ markerboard and markers; chalkboard and chalk; flipchart or overhead projector and transparency
- ❏ flashcards of mission cheer and memory passage
- ❏ mission banks
- ❏ stop watch or watch with second hand
- ❏ paper sack
- ❏ biblical costumes for child shepherd and David
- ❏ staff (stick)
- ❏ guitar
- ❏ paper plates
- ❏ cotton balls
- ❏ bar stool
- ❏ paper sheep
- ❏ markers
- ❏ circles of colored paper, tape
- ❏ notebook of review questions
- ❏ Plasti-Tak® or masking tape

POWer of Worship

Coach's Clipboard (6 minutes)

As winners-in-training, start with a good warm-up exercise. Ask the children to spread out to do jumping jacks, toe-touches, arm/leg circles. Then move them back in beside their chairs and do neck circles, and eye squints to facilitate a calm mood.

Ask the children to be seated. Then do a "brain warm-up" review quiz based on last *kids POWer hour* material. Have a free-for-all. Instruct them to jump up and shout out the answer. There is only one rule: anytime they shout out a wrong answer, they must remain "glued" to their chair when the next question is asked, even if they know the answer. No score is taken, and everyone is placed on his honor to obey the rule. Ten review questions should be sufficient.

Make announcements. Recognize birthdays and introduce guests.

Warm-ups: Sing unto the Lord (8 minutes)

Use the paper sack sheep puppets to encourage the children to sing along. First, let trainers be puppeteers, or do it yourself. Then choose children who are singing "with all their hearts" to be the puppeteers. Start with fun songs the children know.

The man playing the part of David should enter and sit among the children. Do not remark upon his entrance. Let the children wonder. Curiosity is a great attention-getter. Use it often.

Using the pattern on page 126, create this sack puppet. For a more realistic touch, add cotton balls for the "wool," and cut out felt ears, eyes, and nose.

During this series, we will give tips to help your children become acquainted with their Bibles. Knowing God's Word will make them winners!

Trainers should be ready to help those who need it. Encourage preschoolers to flip through their Bibles and "follow along."

Display the first verse of "Amazing Grace." Read it aloud, briefly defining "amazing," "grace," "wretch." Speak the words and do the motions, having the children repeat after you. Then sing "with the spirit and with the understanding." (Save this visual for future use.)

Allow a few minutes for two or three Dynamo Specials.

Exercise: AIM (5 mInutes)

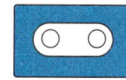 

Call for the AIMer's report.

Lead the children in the mission cheer found on page 12. Use the flashcards from last *kids POWer hour*.

Let children march and sing, "Give and Pray" as they drop their mission offering in a basket or special container. Count the offering immediately and graph it on the offering chart.

Knee Bends: Giving Praise Equal Time (3 minutes)

Often we spend more time asking God for things than we do praising Him. Tell the children that today you are going to give "praise" equal time with prayer. A stop watch or a watch with a second hand is needed. A trainer or older child could be appointed as time keeper.

Take prayer requests. Ask everyone to kneel and lead them in prayer. How long did that take?

Now stand and spend an equal amount of time in praise. Ask the children to raise their hands, clap their hands, give a wave offering. If your children are not acquainted with Pentecostal worship, encourage them to mimic your actions and repeat after you.

Pushups: Testimony Time (3 minutes)

Ask the children to stand and march around the room as the tape plays. When the music stops, each child is to quickly find a seat. After they are seated, ask them to look under their chairs. The ones who find a circle on the bottom of their chair should "push up" and testify.

Pantomime: The Little Lamb (3 minutes)

Play the recording, "The Little Lamb" as the shepherd goes searching for the lamb.

The Good Shepherd provides for and protects His sheep.

Hole for child's arm if desired

POWer of the Word

Training in the Word (5 minutes)

Use the flashcards from last *kids POWer hour* to review the memory passage.

(1) "I will never leave thee, nor forsake thee."
(2) "So that we may boldly say, The Lord is my helper."
(3) "And I will not fear what man shall do unto me" (Hebrews 13:5-6).

What does it mean to be bold? strong, courageous, unafraid

How would you boldly say, "The Lord is my helper, and I will not fear what man shall do unto me"? Would I say it like this? Quote the verse in several ways—a quavery voice, a weak whisper, with a question-

Who Said That?
(3 minutes)

Play the recording of the mystery voices. Instruct the children to listen closely. As you play each one, they are to raise their hand if they think they recognize the speaker. Push the pause button after each speaker to let the children guess. When all have been played, ask: Which one of the speakers is the shepherd of our church?

mark tone. Ask for volunteers to stand and show you how to say it "boldly."

Our enemy, Satan, wants us to be timid and fearful. But we have the weapon of God's Word to make us strong and bold. Let's stand and boldly quote this verse. We want the devil to know that the Lord is our helper and we are not afraid.

Biblical Calisthenics (5 minutes)

We build our spiritual muscles by reading and memorizing God's Word. Let's repeat the spiritual calisthenics we learned last *kids POWer hour*. **Who remembers how to find the Book of Luke?** Let a volunteer come to the front and show how to divide the Bible so that it opens near Luke. (See hour one, page 13, for instructions.) Let the children with Bibles run through this exercise a time or two. Encourage everyone to bring their Bible to *kids POWer hour*.

Who can name the four Gospels? The text we want to read today is found in John. Is that before or after Luke? When you find John 10, raise your hand. As usual, the trainers should move among the children helping where needed.

Read aloud together John 10:11-14.

 Lead the children in a worship chorus to prepare them for the Word of the Lord.

ILLUSTRATED SERMON

David Keeps the Sheep (8 minutes)

The man playing the role of David comes to the front and introduces himself to the coach. The coach expresses surprise at being visited by a king from the Bible. David asks if he can tell his story to the children. The coach responds that they would be happy to hear his story. David uses the script on page 20 as a guide. At the end if the pastor is present, David introduces him. If the pastor is not present, he thanks the coach for letting him tell his story and returns to his seat with the children.

The Shepherd Speaks (8 minutes)

The pastor talks to the children calling them "by name" as much as possible. Allow time for the children to ask questions about what it is like to be the shepherd of the church. Have two or three questions prepared to get the question-answer session started. If it is not possible for the pastor to visit *kids POWer hour*, the coach talks to the children about the pastor's responsibilities. He points out how the pastor as a good shepherd provides and protects his sheep (saints). He concludes by leading them in a prayer for the pastor.

Prayer

Ask the pastor to lay hands on the children with special needs, such as, the Holy Ghost or healing.

Conclude by asking the children to gather around the pastor and pray for him.

Review Game

Bring Them In

Many people do not know like you do that Jesus will be a Shepherd for them and take care of them. That's why it's our responsibility to tell others about Jesus' love.

Tell the group there are (*#'s*) of lost sheep hiding around the room, and they must go find them and bring them back to you. During this time play the *kids POWer hour* tape. Tell the children that when the music stops they must bring their sheep to you and return to their seats.

Give them a few minutes to find them, then stop the tape. Go around the room asking each to name someone they could tell about Jesus. Write that name on one of the sheep and give it to the child as a reminder to tell them about Jesus, the Good Shepherd!

Count the sheep. Were there any sheep not found? Is there time to search again?

Teacher, how sad if we should fail to find one of God's little lambs. We must search diligently.

Give each child a *POWer house* paper as he leaves. Give a missions bank to children who have not received one.

David Keeps the Sheep

David sits on a stool as he talks to the children. He strums his guitar and croons the phrases of Psalm 23. A specific tune is not necessary.

This is my first visit to *kids POWer hour* and what a wonderful time I am having! They didn't have children's church back in Old Testament times when I was a lad. So I just had church by myself. Well, actually, I wasn't alone because all around me were sheep.

Your coach called me a king, and so I was. But I was not always a king and I did not always live in a palace.

I listened to you read about Jesus being our Good Shepherd and how He will never leave us or forsake us. I watched the skit as the shepherd went looking for the lost lamb. All of these brought back so many memories, I just have to tell you my story because long before I was a king, I was a shepherd. I guess God wanted to know if I could be trusted to take care of sheep before He could trust me to take care of His people.

Being a shepherd is a bigger job than most people realize. A shepherd leaves his home and lives wherever there is water and grass for the sheep. He never leaves or forsakes the sheep because their lives depend upon him. Even when wild animals come after the sheep, a true shepherd will not run away. I remember one time when I killed a lion and another time I killed a bear that came after my sheep. I won't tell you that I wasn't afraid, because I was. I was just a boy, and I was horrified. But I loved my sheep and I knew I had to take care of them, even if it cost me my life.

I know what that verse you read in John was talking about when it said that the good shepherd gives his life for his sheep. Jesus did that for us, didn't He?

When you opened your Bibles to the middle, most fell open to the Book of Psalms. Did you know that the Book of Psalms is actually a song book? Many of the psalms are songs that I wrote. Some of them I wrote while I was a young lad sitting on a hillside watching my father's sheep. The best known of the psalms which I wrote is Psalm 23.

One day as I strummed on my harp, these words came to me. I sang, *"The Lord is my shepherd; I shall not want."* Sheep never "want." That means they never worry. They simply follow the shepherd.

"He maketh me to lie down in green pastures; he leadeth me beside the still waters." Sheep do not fret about where they will find water or pasture. They trust the shepherd to find it for them.

"He restoreth my soul: he leadeth me in the paths of righteousness for his name's sake." Did you know that when a sheep gets down on his back, he can't get up by himself? If he lies there very long, he dies. The shepherd has to pick him up and put him back on his feet again. That's what I was talking about when I said the Lord restores our soul. He picks us up and puts us back on our feet when we have been knocked down.

"Yea, though I walk through the valley of the shadow of death, I will fear no evil, for thou art with me." As a shepherd, I took my sheep through many scary places. But not one time did a lamb ever stop and baa, "I'm scared." No. They just followed me where I led. They were not afraid because I was with them.

After I was anointed by the prophet Samuel to be the king of Israel, many frightening things happened to me. But as long as I remembered that the Lord was my shepherd, I was not afraid. The Good Shepherd provides for and protects His sheep.

"Thy rod and thy staff they comfort me." Every shepherd carries a rod which has a crook on the end of it. When a sheep wanders away and falls over a cliff or into a crevice in a rock, the shepherd uses the crook on the end of the rod to reach down and pull the sheep to safety.

"Thou preparest a table before me in the presence of mine enemies: thou anointest my head with oil; my cup runneth over." Shepherds use oil as medicine to anoint the sheep's heads to keep the bugs and insects off and to heal the wounds.

"Surely goodness and mercy shall follow me all the days of my life: and I will dwell in the house of the Lord forever."

Just as I took care of the sheep, I trust the Lord to take care of me. He is my shepherd and I am His sheep.

You have another shepherd the Lord has given you to care for your soul. Do you know who that is? It is your pastor. You are blessed to have a pastor who is willing to give his life to take care of you. Let's all give a big round of applause to Pastor *(name)*.

David exits.

PERMISSION TO COPY

Schedule

Date: _____

I. POWer of Worship (25-30 minutes)
  A. Coach's Clipboard (6 minutes)
    • Brain Warm-up Review Quiz
    • Announcements
  B. Warm-ups: Sing unto the Lord (5 minutes)
  C. Knee Bends: Prayer for Healing (5 minutes)
  D. Exercise: AIM (5 minutes)
  E. Truth Conductor: Disabled (8 minutes)
  F. Pushups: Testimony Time (3 minutes)
II. POWer of the Word (25-30 minutes)
  A. Biblical Calisthenics (3 minutes)
  B. Training in the Word (5 minutes)
    • Unscrambling Hebrews 13:5-6
  C. Spirit Generator (2 minutes)
  D. Illustrated Sermon (15 minutes)
    • Demonstration: Wounded?
    • The Woman with an Infirmity
    • Healed
  E. Invitation and Prayer (5-? minutes)
  F. Review
    • Pass the Torch

 **On Your Mark**

✓ The AIMer for this session should emphasize healing miracles that have taken place in the country which is being spotlighted. Check the *Pentecostal Herald*, *Global Outreach*, and/or the missionary biographies published by Word Aflame Press for testimonies. Make a paper or cloth flag of the country spotlighted for the wall display.

✓ Copy the *POWer house* papers.

✓ Flashcards of the mission cheer and the memory passage are needed.

✓ Write the memory passage, Hebrews 13:5-6, on 3" x 5" cards, one word per card. Make two sets. (Note: only the last phrase of verse 5 is used.)

✓ Place in a box items that help the wounded, *e.g.*, a crutch or cane, sling, ace bandage, ice pack, heating pad, band-aids, etc.

✓ Add true or false review questions based on the last two *kids POWer hours*. Review questions in your notebook can easily be reworded to form true or false statements.

Unit One — A Winning Team—Jesus and Me

Memory Passage: Hebrews 13:5-6

Unit Aim: To help children develop a personal relationship with Jesus Christ.

MY HEALER

The Woman with an Infirmity

Scripture Text: Luke 13:10-17

Jesus heals emotional as well as physical pain.

Supplies

- ❏ *kids POWer hour* tape
- ❏ tape player
- ❏ review question notebook
- ❏ clipboards
- ❏ *POWer house* papers
- ❏ mission banks (for new children)
- ❏ flag of mission country spotlighted
- ❏ "Amazing Grace" visual from last *kids POWer hour*
- ❏ giant marshmallows
- ❏ pretzels
- ❏ blindfolds
- ❏ slings
- ❏ cord or long scarves
- ❏ timer
- ❏ flourescent index cards
- ❏ medical supplies (see items under On Your Mark)
- ❏ band-aids, two per child
- ❏ paper brads for 4-6 year olds *POWer house* activity

PLUG-IN Do your children know why we kneel when we pray? (to acknowledge Jesus as the King of kings) Why do we raise our hands? (in surrender)

Understanding the why's of Pentecostal worship can greater enhance the children's worship. Do not be content only to show them how to worship—tell them why.

POWer of Worship

Coach's Clipboard (6 minutes)

Tell the children that you are going to have a "brain warm-up" exercise. Ask them to stand. If they think the answer to a review statement is "true," they should stand on tiptoe and hold their hands high over their heads. If they think the answer is "false," they should bend over and touch their toes. When the correct answer is given, everyone resumes a normal standing posture and waits for the next question.

Warm-ups: Sing unto the Lord (5 minutes)

"I'm So Glad Jesus Lifted Me"
"Head and Shoulders, Knees and Toes"
"Jesus on the Inside"
"All Things Work Together for Good"
Review "Amazing Grace," using the visual from last *kids POWer hour*.

Knee Bends: Prayer for Healing (5 minutes)

Read Isaiah 53:5 aloud. Then paraphrase: **Jesus was wounded because we sinned. He was bruised because we were wicked. He was punished so we could be free from guilt. He was beaten so we could be healed.** Emphasize God's power to heal.

Mark 16:17-18 says, *"And these signs shall follow them that believe; In my name shall they . . . lay hands on the sick, and they shall recover."* This authorizes believers to lay hands on the sick in Jesus' name. Call for children who need healing to come for prayer. If there is a child with a special need who is not present, ask for someone to stand in as proxy for that child.

Pray and believe.

Ask children who are hurting inside, perhaps their feelings have been hurt or something sad has happened in their family, to raise their hand. Jesus heals emotional as well as physical pain. Lead the children in a prayer for healing of inner pain.

Exercise: AIM (5 minutes)

Call for the AIMer to give his report. Add the flag of that country to the wall display.

Lead the children in the mission cheer and take up the offering. Graph the total. As new children come to *kids POWer hour*, give them mission banks to take home.

Pushups: Testimony Time (3 minutes)

Raise your hand if you have ever been healed by the Lord Jesus. If you would like to share your testimony with us, line up. Let the children use the podium and microphone to testify. If children are reluctant to testify (which is doubtful if they are allowed to use the microphone), start by giving your testimony and asking a trainer or two to give theirs.

POWer of the Word

Biblical Calisthenics (3 minutes)

Everyone who brought a Bible raise it high over your head. Higher. Higher. Stand on tiptoes and hold it as high as you can. Repeat after me: "God's Word is above all other books. It is the greatest book in the world."

Now let's do our biblical calisthenics. Hold your closed Bible between your open palms. How do we find the Book of Psalms? Open the Bible in about the middle. **You may not be in the Book of Psalms, but you will be close.**

How do we find the Gospels? Divide the back half in half. **At the count of three call out the book which you have opened to. Let's see which book we can hear above the others. 1-2-3.** Children should shout out the book their Bibles are opened to. **Which book did you hear?** Be prepared for another loud response.

Our memory passage comes from Hebrews. This New Testament book is a little harder to find. So let's try another trick. Turn to the last book of the Bible. What is it? Revelation. **Now we are going to flip from back to front.** Flip through your Bible as you talk. **Go slowly because the books we will pass getting to Hebrews are small. You will see some familiar names—the names of three of Jesus' disciples, John, Peter, and James. When you see James, stop! Turn slowly, slowly. The book just before James is Hebrews. That is where we are going—Hebrews 13:5-6. Have you found it? Close your Bibles and let's do these biblical calisthenics again.** Lead children through the entire process, starting with the Book of Psalms.

Training in the Word (5 minutes)

Use the memory passage flashcards from last *kids POWer hour* for review.

Divide group into two teams. (For a large group, choose six to eight children for the two teams, or have several teams and sets of cards.) On the count of three, throw the index cards containing words from the memory passage into the air. The teams race to put the passage in order.

ILLUSTRATED SERMON

Wounded? (5 minutes)

Choose a willing "victim." Carry on a dialogue with the children as you patch up the victim's "wounds," using the medical paraphernalia you have collected.

Have you ever been hurt in an accident? What did your mother or the doctor do to help you? Were you prayed for? What happened?

After the victim is patched up, set him in front of the class as a visual.

> Lead the children in a worship chorus magnifying Jesus as the Healer.

> **PLUG-IN** Some translations indicate that this woman's infirmity was emotional, *e.g.*, "a sickness caused by a spirit," "had suffered from a weakening spirit," "had been ill from some psychological cause." Possibly, this woman, like many in our society, was bowed by depression—unable to "lift up herself." Whatever the problem, when Jesus touched her, she was set free and made straight.

The Woman with an Infirmity (4 minutes)

Our sermon today comes from Luke 13. Use our biblical calisthenics to find the Book of Luke. If children need help, go through the Bible flipping process with them.

Follow along as I read from Luke 13, starting with verse 13.

"And he [Jesus] was teaching in one of the synagogues [Jewish churches] on the sabbath [the Jews' day to go to church].

"And, behold, there was a woman which had a spirit of infirmity [a crippling sickness] eighteen years, and was bowed together [bent over], and could in no wise lift up herself."

Eighteen years is a long time to be bent double. Everyone, please, stand. Bend over and touch your toes. Do not straighten up until I say you can. Slowly count to eighteen. **Now you can straighten up and be seated. That was only eighteen seconds! How would it feel if you were bent double for eighteen years—that's longer than you are old.** Let children respond.

One day something wonderful happened! This crippled woman met Jesus at church. Let's read, starting with verse 12.

"And when Jesus saw her, he called her to him, and said unto her, "Woman, thou art loosed from thine infirmity."

"And he laid hands on her."

What do you think happened when Jesus laid His hands on the crippled woman? Girls, read the rest of that verse aloud.

"And immediately she was made straight, and glorified God."

Crack! Pop! Snap! The bones in this woman's back that had been locked in curves started unlocking. Suddenly, the woman realized she could stand straight and tall—for the first time in eighteen years!

Everyone, please, stand again. Imagine you are the woman with the infirmity who has been healed. Your back has just been straightened after *how many years of being bent double*? What would you do?

Here's what I think I would do. And I think you would, too. So do what I do. Okay?  As you do the following, the children mimic your actions.

I would carefully hold my shoulders as straight and high as I could. I would run my hand up and down my spine to see if it was straight. I would lift one shoulder, then the other, again and again. Feel my spine one more time. Then slowly, oh so slowly, and carefully, I would bend over—just a little bit in case something might lock up again. Then I would straighten up, twist my shoulders, feel my spine. Take a deep breath and smile. Then I would bend—way over—touch my toes, straighten up. Raise my hands, jump for joy, and shout, "Hallelujah! I've been healed. Oh, thank You, Jesus." And I would smile and laugh and jump and spin around and clap my hands for joy.

Let's all clap our hands for Jesus, our Healer. Lead children in a round of applause.

Healed (6 minutes)

Ask the children to be seated. Choose volunteers to pass out the band-aids. Give each child two.

Do you have a wound on your hand or leg which needs a band-aid? If so, put a band-aid on it. If you do not have one, pretend that you have one on the back of your hand and put a band-aid on it. Use only

> **PLUG-IN** As the Illustrated Sermon is given, a trainer could be adding review questions to the notebook.

one of your band-aids. Trainers should move among the children helping the smaller ones and picking up the wrappings.

Wounds like these are called "physical hurts" because they happen to our body. We take care of them with band-aids, slings, and medicine. Jesus heals physical wounds. Sometimes He gives us a miracle and heals us instantly. Other times He lets the healing process He built into our bodies work and heal us. However He chooses to do it, Jesus is the Healer.

There are other kinds of wounds that hurt just as bad as a cut or burn or break. These are "emotional wounds." They are like inward bruises. These hurt our hearts and make us cry. They hurt our feelings. Unwrap your other band-aid and put it over your heart to represent the things which wound us inside. What are some things that hurt our feelings, that bruise us inside? Answers could include: unkind words, rejection by friends or family, abuse, name-calling, mean jokes, divorce of parents, friends moving away, being laughed at.

These things hurt your heart as much as if someone were throwing rocks at you, or stabbing you with a knife. Jesus came to be your heart healer, too. He heals emotional as well as physical pain.

Jesus understands when you tell Him your feelings. People hurt Him too, so He knows what it feels like. He understands your pain, whether it is physical or emotional—inside or out—and He wants to heal you.

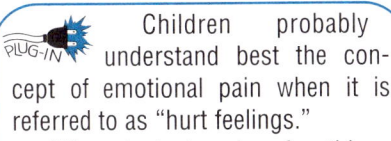

Children probably understand best the concept of emotional pain when it is referred to as "hurt feelings."

When brainstorming for things which wound us, take seriously each thing named by the children, even though it may seem "childish" to you. Remember you are dealing with children with tender hearts. It does not take much to hurt them.

Invitation and Prayer (5-? minutes)

As the musician plays, call for the children who are hurting, whether it is from a physical wound, a sickness, or an emotional problem to come to the front for prayer. Ask the trainers to gather around and pray with these children.

Conclude the prayer by asking the children to raise their hands and praise the Lord for healing them. Then have them remove the band-aids as a symbol of their healing. Ask one of the trainers to remove the bandages, splints, etc., from the "victim."

Review

Assign each child a teammate. Everyone sits or stands in a circle, with teams together. As the music plays, the children pass the Olympic torch around the circle. When the music stops, the child holding the torch is asked a review question. He consults with his teammate before answering. If he misses, he drops out. Continue until only one team is left.

For variety, the children could quote a Bible verse or name a Bible character.

If there is time, help the 4-6 year olds cut out and put together the woman with the infirmity in their *POWer house* paper. If there is not time, give each one paper brads in a small envelope, as few people have paper brads at home.

Give each child a *POWer house* paper as they leave.

A Note to the Music Director

As you sing the old familiar hymns and praise choruses in adult church, listen for words or phrases which might be perplexing to children. Make notes of these.

Each *kids POWer hour* sing one of these songs, defining the words and explaining the meaning of the phrases in simple terms.

It is not enough for our children to sing, they need to sing "with the spirit and with the understanding." The spirit comes from God; the understanding comes from us.

Unit One   **A Winning Team—Jesus and Me**

My Savior

The Samaritan Woman Meets the Savior

Memory Passage: Hebrews 13:5-6

Unit Aim: To help children develop a personal relationship with Jesus Christ.

Scripture Text: John 4

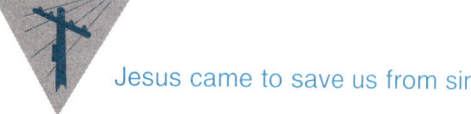

Jesus came to save us from sin.

Schedule

Date: _____

I. POWer of Worship (25-30 minutes)
   A. Coach's Clipboard (6 minutes)
      • Announcements
      • Puppet Review Quiz
   B. Warm-ups: Sing unto the Lord (6 minutes)
   C. Exercise: AIM (5 minutes)
   D. Knee Bends: Prayer (4 minutes)
   E. Truth Conductor: What Is It?
      (4 minutes)
   F. Pushups: V-I-C-T-O-R-Y (4 minutes)
II. POWer of the Word (25-30 minutes)
   A. Biblical Calisthenics (5 minutes)
      • Scripture Drill
   B. Training in the Word (8 minutes)
      • "Outnumbered"
   C. Spirit Generator (2 minutes)
   D. Illustrated Sermon (7 minutes)
      • A Sinful Woman Meets the Savior
   E. Invitation and Prayer (5-? minutes)
   F. Review
      • Move Up

 **On Your Mark**

✓ The AIMer's report should zero in on revival in a foreign land. Sources of information are missionary biographies published by Word Aflame Press, *The Pentecostal Herald*, *Global Outreach*, and letters from your church's partners-in-missions. Make a flag for the missions display.

✓ Copy the *POWer house* papers, the story, "Outnumbered," and the monologue of the woman at the well.

✓ Read the introductory page for Unit Two (page 32). A man or older teen needs to be chosen to play the role of Professor N. A. Dither. Give him copies of his scripts for hours 5-9 at one time to give him a better picture of his character. He can carry a copy of the script on a clipboard. He needs to be familiar enough with it that he does not appear to read it. As in all skits, he needs to be given freedom to ad lib and add creativity to the role. (If a man is not available, a puppet can be used. In this case, a puppeteer needs to be chosen and prepared for the part.)

✓ For each child you need five small paper hearts, one black, one red, one white, one brown, and one gold foil or yellow. Punch a hole in the top of each and put them together with yarn—in the order listed—to make a songbook. As the children enter, give each a mini-songbook and ask them to loop the yarn around a button. This will keep the book handy while leaving their hands free. On large hearts of the same colors, write the words to the song, "My Heart Was Black as Sin," for a visual.

> Black heart: **My heart was black as sin**
> Red heart: **Until the Savior came in.**
> **His precious blood I know**
> White heart: **Has made me white as snow.**
> Brown heart: **And in His Word I'm told**
> Gold foil/ yellow heart: **I'll walk on streets of gold.**
> **Oh, wonderful, wonderful day!**
> **He washed my sins away.**

✓ Add questions on this lesson to your review notebook. This can be done before children's church or by a trainer during the service.
✓ Write sins, such as lying, cheating, stealing, hate, pride, on small slips of paper. Roll up and insert each in a balloon. Inflate the balloons and tie off. For a small group, have one balloon per child. Display the balloons in the front of the room for attention getters.
✓ Label seven opaque glasses of water with a foreign word for "water," *e.g.*, "agua" (Spanish); "mizu" (Japanese); "pani" (Urdu spoken in Pakistan); "voda" (Russian); "wasser" (German); "l'eau" (French), and "tubig" (Tagalog spoken in the Philippines). Before the children arrive, fill the glasses with water. To add to the challenge, add a few drops of food coloring to some of the glasses.
✓ With a copy machine enlarge the art of the dogs on page 30. Color and cut out. Glue each to a craft stick. These signs are used to involve the children in the practical story, "Outnumbered."
✓ Give a copy of the monologue to "the woman at the well." She wears a simple biblical robe and carries a bucket with some water in it. The script is not intended to be memorized, merely used as a guide.
✓ Pile bricks or heavy stones (one for each child) just inside the door.

Supplies

- ❏ *kids POWer hour* tape
- ❏ tape player
- ❏ review notebook
- ❏ *POWer house* papers
- ❏ clipboards
- ❏ copies of Professor N. A. Dither's scripts from Unit Two
- ❏ copies of "Outnumbered"
- ❏ construction paper or posterboard, black, red, white, brown, yellow (or gold foil)
- ❏ yarn
- ❏ markers
- ❏ flag of mission country
- ❏ bricks or rocks, one per child
- ❏ balloons
- ❏ puppet
- ❏ seven opaque glasses of water
- ❏ labels for glasses
- ❏ food coloring
- ❏ enlarged art of dog (see margin)
- ❏ three craft sticks
- ❏ biblical costume for Samaritan woman
- ❏ copy of monologue
- ❏ bucket containing some water

POWer of Worship

Coach's Clipboard (6 minutes)

Let's start this *kids POWer hour* with a bang. Call for a child to come to the front and burst a balloon. Collect the slip from the balloon. **Look what was in the balloon.** Read aloud the word on the slip. **I wonder what that is all about?** Put the paper in your Bible.

Make announcements. Acknowledge birthdays and welcome guests.

For a review quiz over last *kids POWer hour*, have a free-for-all with a puppet as the quiz master. Ask riddles along with the questions to keep the kids laughing—and listening.

What has hands but cannot clap for Jesus? a clock
What animal does not play fair? a cheetah
What would a home be without children? quiet

Tell the children the *POWer line*: **Jesus came to save us from sin.** Have them repeat it after you several times. Tell them to remember it because they will need it later. Each time the *POWer line* is repeated, burst a balloon. Read the slip to the children, then put it in your Bible.

Warm-ups: Sing unto the Lord (6 minutes)

"Mine, Mine, Mine, Jesus Is Mine"
"I Love Him Better Every D-A-Y"
"Happy All the Time"

Children love to burst balloons. If it is not too disruptive, call a different child to burst one each time the *POWer line* is read.

"My Heart was Black as Sin" (Use the illustrated song and the mini-songbooks to teach this song. Children turn the pages in their books as the leader turns the pages in the illustrated song.)

Dynamo Specials

Always make time for specials from the children. Make participation, not perfection, the goal. A hearty round of applause is a great confidence builder.

Exercise: AIM (5 minutes)

Lead the children in the mission cheer. Call for the AIMer's report and add the country's flag to the wall display.

Take the offering and graph it on the chart. How are you coming on your project? Give yourself a round of applause.

Knee Bends: A Prayer for Salvation (4 minutes)

Read aloud Isaiah 45:22 from your Bible. *"Look unto me, and be ye saved, all the ends of the earth: for I am God, and there is none else."* People from the North, South, East, and West can look to Jesus and be saved. Salvation is for "all men, women, boys, and girls everywhere." Jesus came to save us from sin. Burst another balloon.

Divide the children into four groups, north, south, east, and west. Each group is to turn the direction they have been given and pray for the salvation of people around your church. (Or this prayer could be expanded to reach around the world.)

What Is It? (4 minutes)

Draw children's attention to the labeled glasses of water.

Have you ever drank "mizu"? Call for a volunteer to taste it. **What does it taste like?**

Repeat this with each glass. How long does it take them to catch on that each glass contains water?

Water is one thing everyone must have to live. Winners-in-training need lots of water. Discuss how athletes and people who are working hard in hot weather need lots of water. **All water is life-giving, but Jesus gives us living water. What is living water? We will soon know.**

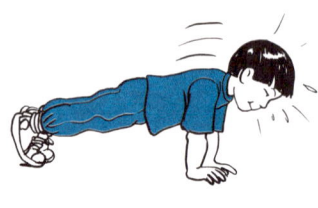

Pushups: V-I-C-T-O-R-Y (4 minutes)

Read Revelation 12:11 to the children. *"And they overcame him [Satan] by the blood of the Lamb, and by the word of their testimony."*

The "blood of the Lamb" is referring to Jesus' death on the cross. By the blood Jesus shed for us on the cross and by the word of our testimony, we can defeat the devil. We are winners!

Lead the children in this rousing cheer of victory!
V-I-C-T-O-R-Y, That's the Christian battle cry!
V-I-C-T-O-R-Y, vic-tor-y for you and I!
After each testimony, let the children repeat the cheer.
What is the *POWer line*? Jesus came to save us from our sins. Burst a balloon.

POWer of the Word

Biblical Calisthenics (5 minutes)

Do you remember how to do your biblical calisthenics to find Hebrews? Call for a volunteer to come to the front and show the class how. If no one can remember, lead them though the Bible flipping steps given in the last *kids POWer hour*.

To build mental muscles, let's have a short Scripture drill using the steps we have learned. When you find the verse, jump to your feet, but do not read until three others are on their feet. All four will read together. As these verses are read, everyone listen for the key word. This is an important word which will be in every verse; it is also in the *POWer line*. Do you remember the *POWer line*? Jesus came to save us from sin. Burst another balloon. **When you think you know the key word, raise your hand.**

References: Psalm 54:1, 20:9; 69:1; Matthew 1:21; Luke 19:10; Hebrews 7:25. Key Word: save.

Now let's find and read together Hebrews 13:5-6.

Training in the Word (8 minutes)

Ask those who can quote Hebrews 13:5-6 to line up (or simply stand).

The first child says the first word, the second child says the next, and so on down the line and back again until the entire passage has been quoted. Give them a round of applause as they return to their seats.

What does this verse mean? Let two or three children respond. Thank them for their answers, even if they are not exactly right.

The story, "Outnumbered," will help us understand why we do not have to be afraid when the Lord is with us.

The story "Outnumbered" is found on page 30.

Questions for discussion: **Do you ever feel like Rusty, outnumbered and jumped on by everyone? How can God help us when we are outnumbered? Why do we not have to be afraid of people? What is the *POWer line*? Jesus came to save us from our sins.**  A savior is one who saves another. Bud was Rusty's savior. Jesus Christ is our Savior because He saves us from the penalty of sin. Burst another balloon and collect the paper from it. Read aloud all the slips from the balloons collected to this point. Appear puzzled as to what the connection is between these words. Ask the children if they have any idea. Listen to their suggestions and comment: **You might be right. Surely we will find out before this service is over.**

Ask the children to stand and stretch. Then as the music plays, have them march around the room and pick up a brick or rock from the pile. After they pick up their weight, they should return to their seats. Tell them to hold the brick on their lap until you tell them they may put it down. Trainers should sit among the children, making sure that the bricks are not mishandled.

Worship Chorus

Lead the children in a quiet worship chorus to prepare for the Word of the Lord.

Assign this story to a trainer to read. The reader should show emotion in both his voice and body language. Involve the children in the story by assigning them parts.
• The 4-5 year olds are Rusty, the cocker spaniel.
• The 6-8 year olds are the pack of dogs, represented by the mutt.
• The 9-11 years olds are Bud, the boxer.

When the picture of their dog is held up, the children bark and growl. Before reading the story, give the instructions and hold up each picture for the children to practice. At one time everyone is barking so the reader will have to be loud to be heard. If your group is large, you may need to limit the "barkers" to smaller groups, such as, the first grade or fourth row. The instant a picture is put down, the "dogs" stop barking.

Outnumbered

Darren threw his books on the bed and plopped down beside them. Mr. Marland stopped at the door. "Anything wrong?"

Looking at his toes, Darren nodded. Mr. Marland came in and sat down beside the boy. He put his arm around his son's shoulder. "Want to tell me about it?"

"Oh, Dad, I'm just sick of school! You ought to hear those kids talk. They cuss and cut people down and tell filthy jokes. They call me a nerd and a wimp because I don't act like they do. I'd like to punch Jeff and Ted in the nose. I'm just sick of it all."

Mr. Marland tightened his grip of Darren's shoulders. "I know, son, but you can't. . . ."

Darren continued, "I'm the only kid in my class who even tries to be a Christian. Please, Dad, couldn't I go to a Christian school?"

"I wish you could, son," his dad sighed, "but you know the nearest one is forty miles away. And, besides, we can't afford the tuition."

Darren rubbed his eyes with the back of his hand. "I know, Dad. I didn't mean to whine. Some days are worse than others. I'll. . . ."

Hold up picture of cocker spaniel. ***Arf-arf! Growwwwwl! Yap-yap!*** "That sounds like Rusty!" Darren jumped to his feet. "He's hurt." He ran down the hall, followed by Mr. Marland. Hold up picture of mutt. **"It's not just one dog, Dad. It sounds like a pack."**

Darren ran out on the porch. "It is! They've got Rusty. They're going to kill him!" He bounded down the steps.

"Stop, Darren!" Mr. Marland ordered. "You'll get hurt." Mr. Marland ran for the garage. "I'll get the baseball bat."

Hold up picture of boxer. ***GRRRRROWL!*** **A huge growl chilled the air as their neighbor's boxer, Bud, came running down the street and jumped into the middle of the fight. Dogs scattered everywhere.** Put down picture of mutt.

"Look, Dad. Look!" Darren pointed in amazement. "Bud is fighting Rusty's battle."

Put down cocker spaniel and boxer signs. **The big dog stood protectively over the little cocker spaniel as he picked himself up.** Put up cocker spaniel sign. **Rusty looked up at his deliverer and whined.** Put down cocker spaniel sign and put up boxer. **Bud gently nudged the little dog toward home.** Put down boxer sign.

Mr. Marland shook his head in wonder as Darren knelt beside the limping pup. Put up cocker spaniel sign. **Rusty whimpered as Bud turned and walked proudly down the street.** Put down cocker spaniel sign. **Darren chuckled, "You've got yourself some friend, Rusty."**

Mr. Marland put his hand on his boy's shoulder. Darren looked up. "And so do you, son. You may be outnumbered at school, but you've got a Friend who makes up the difference."

Darren grinned, "You mean God?"

Mr. Marland nodded.

Darren stood up with Rusty in his arms. "Thanks, Dad, for reminding me. I think I'll just let God fight my battles. Sure helps to have a big friend, huh, Rusty?"

taken from *Rhymes, Riddles and Reasons*
by Barbara Westberg, Published by Word Aflame Press
Used by permission
PERMISSION TO COPY THIS PAGE

Invitation and Prayer
(5-? minutes)

The brick (rock) you are holding is like sin. It's heavy, and the longer you carry it, the heavier it gets.

You do not have to answer this question aloud or raise your hand. Have you ever done something wrong for which you are ashamed? Sure you have. We all have. Didn't it make you feel heavy and sad inside? That's the guilt of sin. The longer you carry it, the heavier it gets.

Jesus came to save you from sin. Call children to burst the remaining balloons. Collect the slips and read them to the children. What are these things I have read? Sins. **These sins will make you feel guilty and ashamed—heavy inside.**

Musician plays.

Jesus is our Savior. Bud saved Rusty from the pack of dogs. Jesus wants to save you from your sins. He wants to take away the heavy, ugly feeling inside you and give you living water—His Spirit—that will make you bubble with joy.

I do not know your heart, but Jesus does. If you want to be happy and free from sin, come to the front and put down your brick. When you do this, you will show Jesus that you are sorry and want Him to fill you with the Holy Ghost.

After prayer, sing again "My Heart Was Black as Sin," using the mini-songbooks.

Review

Place four chairs in front of the class. Ask four volunteers to be the first quiz panel. If the player answers correctly, he stays on the panel. If he answers incorrectly, he is out and chooses another child to take his place.

Give each child a *POWer house* paper as he leaves.

ILLUSTRATED SERMON

Monologue: The Woman at the Well (7 minutes)

The "Samaritan woman" enters and tells her story as a monologue.

A Sinful Woman Meets the Savior

Woman enters, wearing a biblical robe and carrying a bucket with some water in it. Talks as she walks up the aisle and takes a seat in front of the class.

Hello, kids. Thank you for letting me come to *kids POWer hour*. I understand that you are winners-in-training. I am a winner, too, but I haven't always been. For many years I was a loser—a big time loser.

I am from a country in Bible days called Samaria. Before I met Jesus, I lived a very sinful life. Nothing made me happy. I was married five times. I was always looking for happiness, but never finding it. I felt dry and empty inside.

I was so embarrassed by my sinful life that it was hard to meet people, and often people shunned me.

In fact, the day my life was changed—the day I met Jesus—I had gone to the well to draw water. Motions to bucket. Everybody in our community got their water at the well. We did not have it piped into our houses like you do. Most of the women went to the well in the morning or evening when it was cool. So I went at noon, thinking that no one would be there.

But, alas, when I got to the well, Jesus was there. He asked me for a drink. I was shocked! He was a Jew, and I was a Samaritan. Jews did not talk to Samaritans. They thought they were better than we were and wanted nothing to do with us. Usually, they traveled miles out of their way to keep from passing through our country. It was unusual to see a Jew in our community. I understood how it felt to be shunned and ignored, but I had trouble accepting acceptance.

Jesus actually wanted to talk to me. I could not believe it. He told me about the sin in my life. He understood how miserable and ashamed I was. He offered me "living water."

Living water is not like this water. Put hand in the bucket and splash a few drops. This water refreshes your mouth when you are thirsty. Living water is a feeling inside that makes you happy and bubbly. I was lonely and full of guilt. How I wanted to be joyful and bubbly. The living water Jesus was talking about is His Spirit.

I was so excited about meeting the Savior, the One who could take away my sins and give me living water, that I ran back into the city and told everyone, "Come see the Man who told me everything I had ever done."

When you meet Jesus, the first thing you want to do is tell others about Him. Meeting Jesus changed me from a loser to a winner—a soul winner.

Stands. If you haven't met Jesus, I hope you will meet Him today. Why be a loser when you can be a winner?

Exits.

PERMISSION TO COPY

Unit Two　　　　　　　　　　　　　　　　　　　　　　　　　**In Training**

Self-Esteem

Memory Passage: Philippians 4:13

Unit Aim: To help children realize their potential in Christ.

Each child in your *kids POWer hour* is a possibility. He can possibly become a mighty soul winner, taking hundreds to heaven with him. Or he can become a drug pusher, making life on earth a hell for hundreds. He can fill a pulpit or prison cell. He has the potential to be the best of the best or the worst of the worst.

This unit is designed to build the children's self-esteem, not to make them arrogant, but to develop their potential for Christ. Few children in this day think more highly of themselves than they ought. Most are tormented with feelings of insecurity and inferiority.

Far too many are verbally, as well as physically, abused and kicked down by parents who also are tormented by insecurity and inferiority.

Often the child who is the most abrasive is the one who is the most insecure. If we are not sensitive to the Spirit of the Lord, we may mislabel this child as a "braggart and smart aleck." When, actually, he is simply a hurting, fear-filled kid.

Each of the Bible characters studied the next five *POWer hours* had abilities and disabilities. We will point out to the children how the disabilities became stepping stones as they, along with the abilities, were yielded to God.

This unit gives the teacher an opportunity to do something truly special—show the children their talents. Helping a child develop his talents is one of the greatest challenges of teaching.

Introducing

Professor N. A. Dither

Professor N. A. Dither lives up to his name. He comes into the classroom flustered and he leaves flustered.

From his rambling exhortations, the children learn as they laugh.

The man or teen boy who plays this part should be uninhibited and creative. Help him assemble his costume, and give him copies of his scripts early so he can be well prepared.

Change the look of your room for this unit. Enlarge the art of the professor from the back of this manual onto foamcore or cardboard to make a full-size stand-up figure. Move in a desk and place the professor beside it. Display a banner, "Training in Progress." Keep the gym equipment, but rearrange it.

Schedule

Date:_____
I. POWer of Worship (25-30 minutes)
   A. Coach's Clipboard (6 minutes)
      • Welcoming Activities
      • Professor N. A. Dither
      • Announcements
   B. Warm-ups (5 minutes)
      • Sing unto the Lord
      • Dynamo Specials
   C. Knee Bends (3 minutes)
      • Heart Exercise
   D. Pushups (8 minutes)
      • Puppet Skit
   E. Exercise: AIM (5 minutes)
      • Missions Report
      • Offering
II. POWer of the Word (25-30 minutes)
   A. Training in the Word (4 minutes)
      • An Exercise in Futility
   B. Biblical Calisthenics (3 minutes)
      • Biblical Calisthenics
   C. Spirit Generator (2 minutes)
   D. Illustrated Sermon (8 minutes)
      • Miriam, Leader of the Rhythm Band
   E. Truth Conductor (5 minutes)
      • Lighting the Olympic Torch
   F. Invitation and Prayer (5-? minutes)
   G. Review Game

 **On Your Mark**

✓ Make time this week to coordinate your plans with "Professor N. A. Dither" whether he is played by a man or a puppeteer. He should have been given copies of the script last *kids POWer hour* and be prepared to get down to the nitty-gritty of the role.

✓ The AIMer's report should spotlight a specific missionary, preferably one of your church's PIM's. Talk about how God has blessed this "ordinary" person with "extraordinary gifts," beginning with the gift of the Holy Ghost. Any of the missionary biographies published by Word Aflame Press could be used here.

✓ Cut a sheet of posterboard in half to make the covers for a giant book. Use art paper for the pages. Design a cover for "The Life of Miriam." Inside pages are titled, "Chapter One: Deliverance on the Water," and "Chapter Two: Deliverance on Dry Ground." A copy of the Illustrated Sermon may be taped onto the pages for a guide. Choose an older girl to play the part of Miriam. Run though the text with her beforehand. If you do not have the *kids POWer hour* tape, prerecord the text found in the margin on page 38.

Unit Two — **In Training**

Memory Verse: Philippians 4:13

Unit Aim: To help children realize their potential in Christ.

I Am Gifted

Miriam, Leader of the Rhythm Band

Scripture Text: Exodus 2:1-10, 15:20-21; Romans 12:6-8; Luke 11:11-13; James 1:1-17

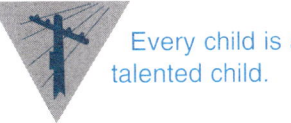 Every child is a gifted and talented child.

Supplies

- ❏ *kids POWer hour* tape
- ❏ tape player
- ❏ *POWer house* papers
- ❏ blank tape
- ❏ copies of scripts
- ❏ Professor N. A. Dither's costume
- ❏ clipboards
- ❏ exercise equipment, preferably weights
- ❏ puppets
- ❏ school books
- ❏ muscle-building book or manual for exercise equipment
- ❏ posterboard
- ❏ markers
- ❏ art paper
- ❏ markerboard
- ❏ simple robe for Miriam
- ❏ doll wrapped in blanket
- ❏ tambourine
- ❏ candles, several smaller tapers and one large pillar candle
- ❏ matches
- ❏ review notebook
- ❏ gray or brown posterboard
- ❏ clear contact paper for laminating stones
- ❏ Plasti-Tak®
- ❏ plastic bag

✓ Assemble materials.
✓ Decide if you are going to use puppets in the Pushups segment or have the trainers tell about their gifts. Dialogue (whether puppets or in person) could be something like: "I have a gift for making friends. I like people, and they like me." "I am good at making things. I made a bird house that my dad said was as good as he could make." "I have a gift for music. I love to play the guitar and my teacher said I have exceptional talent." Make a list of things children might do well, *e.g.,* helping, baby sitting, running errands, reading, writing, art, math, praying, singing.
✓ Choose a small, unathletic-type helper (can be male or female) to portray the part of someone unsuccessfully trying to exercise using weights or other equipment. (A jump rope will do if nothing else is available.) Give him a copy of the script so he can be prepared.
✓ For the review game make an assortment of stone shapes from gray or brown posterboard rock. (How many depends upon the size of the room and the number of children.) After laminating them, write "yes," on half and "no," on the other half. Use Plasti-Tak® to place stones in a hodge-podge fashion around the room to make a path.
✓ Add questions over this lesson to the review notebook. Word them so they can be answered, "yes" or "no." If more questions are needed for the game, reword questions from past *kids POWer hours* so they can be answered with "yes" and "no."

POWer of Worship

Coach's Clipboard (6 minutes)

Welcome to *kids POWer hour* **Olympic Training Camp. I'm Coach** *(name).* **We are here to exercise our bodies, minds, and souls. First, a little brain exercise. Repeat after me:** Every child is a gifted and talented child. **This is our** *POWer line.* **Tuck it in your brain.** Pretend to do so. **Each time I flex my muscles in the "power signal," I want you to yell out the** *POWer line.* Flex muscles. Children should respond.

Welcome guests and introduce them to the children.

Let's get on with our workout. Ask the children to spread out and do a few simple breathing and movement activities for one minute or less.

Our whole body benefits from exercising. Our brain functions better when we exercise. How many need their brain to function better? Raise your hand. **Speaking of brains** (look around cautiously before continuing), **from time to time we will leave the gym here and go to other places on campus. We may pop into Professor N. A. Dither's classroom. He is quite a** (hesitate) **a . . . a . . . a brain. You'll see what I mean when he tries to teach his class. He's got what he calls "brain food."**

Professor N A. Dither enters, stumbling along with an armload of books, mumbling to himself.

COACH:	**Oh, speaking of being "out to lunch," here's the professor himself. Why, good morning, Professor.**
PROFESSOR:	Startled. **H-H-Hello, Coach. Where'd you come from? I thought you worked in the gym.**
COACH:	**That's correct. But, we are in the gym, Professor.**
PROFESSOR:	Looks around. Confused. **Oh, y-y-yes. It is, isn't it? I must have been thinking of Amy and taken a wrong turn.** Continues to be disoriented.

COACH: Smiles and winks at children. **Amy? Is she your new girlfriend, Professor?**

PROFESSOR: **No, no, no. I don't have time for girlfriends. I'm on my way back to my office to grade these exams. I'm always buried in paperwork. Amy is one of my nuclear physics students. She is about to flunk this semester. She left the classroom in tears when I broke the news to her about her grade average.**

COACH: **Nuclear physics? That sounds tough, Professor. I don't know that I could do much better myself. How about you, boys and girls? How many of you are whizzes in science?** Raises hand to indicate response wanted. **Is there any hope for her, Professor? I mean, can we** (motion to self and audience) **be of any help?**

PROFESSOR: **It's a tough case, Coach. She said she was also failing her other two physics classes.**

COACH: **Hmmm, it sounds bad. What is her problem? Doesn't she take notes and study?**

PROFESSOR: **Oh, yes, yes. She tries harder than anyone else in the class. But when it comes to science, she just doesn't have it up here.** Points to head. **You know, she just can't seem to digest that "brain food."**

COACH: Whispers aside to audience. **See, I told you about the "brain food."** To Professor. **She's pretty blue right now, huh?**

PROFESSOR: **Oh, yes. Blue? Yes, she's blue all right.** Mutters as he exits. **I've done everything possible to help the child, but she just doesn't have it up here** (points to head). **Yes, she is blue.**

PERMISSION TO COPY SCRIPT

Warm-ups: Sing unto the Lord (5 minutes)

Let's sing some songs to cheer ourselves up. We don't want to be blue, do we?
"I'm So Happy"
"The Joy of the Lord is my Strength"

Dynamo Specials

Plan ahead of time to have an instrumentalist or vocalist from your children's church audience perform during this time. Set a time limit for them so they can practice with that in mind. Amateurs may take more time than they realize.

Knee Bends: Prayer (3 minutes)

Did you know that prayer is exercise? No, not of your vocal chords to see who can pray the loudest. It is fine to pray loud; in fact, sometimes we become so intense, we just have to pray in a loud voice. But God hears the quietest prayer—if it comes from the heart. One woman in the Bible was so heart-broken that she could not even utter a sound when she prayed. She simply moved her lips. Do you know who she was? Hannah. Why was she heart-broken? She wanted a child. God answered her prayer, even though she did not say a word, because it came from her heart. God heard the cry of her heart.

Prayer is spiritual heart exercise. My heart, not the one that goes thump-thump, but the depths of my emotions—how I feel deep down inside me—that heart is flexing its muscles when I pray.

Today we are going to do our spiritual heart exercises. I want you to stand and close your eyes. Think of something you need to tell the Lord or ask Him. Allow a few seconds for children to think. While the musician plays a chorus softly, we are going to pray silently. You can

move your lips if you want to, but do not pray aloud. Pray from your heart. Are you ready?

Musician plays a chorus. When music stops, everyone says, "Amen" and opens their eyes.

Pushups: Lifting Up One Another (8 minutes)

During testimony time, we can help "push up" or "lift up" the Lord as we praise Him. We can make ourselves feel better, as well as others, by testifying of what God has done for us.

I just can't get poor Amy off my mind. I feel that if she would switch majors, to maybe math, or music, or something else that she can do well in, she would succeed. I have heard that she can solve those complicated equations in algebra and trigonometry classes. She even tutors students in the evenings who are having trouble. She needs to concentrate on what she is gifted in, even though she would like to do well in science. Maybe no one has ever told Amy. . . . Flex muscles. Children should respond. **Every child is a gifted and talented child.**

We have often been under the impression that if we admit we can do something well, we are bragging on ourselves. That's not the case. Let's watch our friends as they show us a positive way to look at our gifts.

Do a short puppet skit, or have trainers who have a good self-concept and realize their strong points briefly tell what they are good at doing.

Boys and girls, I'd like for you to think of two things you can do well. As I read things children can do, when I say one you feel you are good at, raise your hand. This will not mean you are bragging. It just shows that you realize your gift. Jesus can use your gift if you allow him to. He is the one who has given it to you.

Flex muscle. **Every child is a gifted and talented child.**

Exercise: AIM (5 minutes)

AIMer gives his report on an ordinary person who with God's gifts, including receiving the Holy Ghost, became an extraordinary missionary.

Take the offering and graph it on the chart.

POWer of the Word

Training in the Word (4 minutes)

A prechosen person, carrying an exercise manual and a Bible, comes to the front and starts exercising. From time to time he refers to the manual, and then the Bible, before going back to exercising.

Approach this person and call him by name several times before he responds.

TRAINER: Pants. **Oh, hi, coach.** Wipes brow as he talks.
COACH: **Trying to get in shape for the *kids POWer hour* Olympics?**
TRAINER: Picks up manual. **I'm trying to look like this.** Shows coach. Flexes muscles. **Just think how strong and muscular I'll be in another week—if I can figure out how to get these things off the floor.** Refers to weights or adapts to fit equipment.

 **PLUG-IN** When the trainer flexes his muscles, some of the children may respond with the *POWer line*. If so, the coach and trainer should smile and nod agreement. A comment like, "Boy, you kids are on the ball," would not distract from the action.

The dialogue in this material is given for a guide, not to restrict interaction with the children. Be flexible, even though the text is engraved on the page.

	Picks up Bible and opens to Philippians 4:13. **Right here, Coach, God's Word promises me I'll be able to do it.**
COACH:	**The Bible promises you will develop muscles in a week? Let me see that.** Trainer gives the coach the Bible. He reads. *"I can do all things through Christ which strengtheneth me."*
TRAINER:	Answers smugly as he goes back to exercising. **Yep. I can do all these things with a little more practice because they will strengthen me.** Continues to exercise while coach talks to the children.
COACH:	**We can always believe the Bible. But we need to ask for guidance and wisdom when studying it.** Picks up exercise manual. **Advertisements can be misleading. God's Word is never misleading, but it is possible to read into it something that is not there.** **We exercise to keep our bodies healthy. But there are certain limitations we have to observe. God has laws which apply to our bodies. They grow in certain ways and at certain times. We do not develop muscles overnight or even in a week. That is not the way God designed our bodies.** **God's Word never goes against God's laws—because God's Word is the basis for His laws.** **When we read,** *"I can do all things through Christ which strengtheneth me,"* **we are limited to the bounds of God's laws. Jesus will not help us do anything that breaks His laws.**

PERMISSION TO COPY SCRIPT

Ask the children to applaud the trainer as he returns to his seat.

Biblical Calisthenics (3 minutes)

Write "Philippians 4:13" on a board so the children can see how it is spelled and recognize it in their Bibles.

Quickly run though the biblical calisthenics learned in past *kids POWer hours*. When they find Hebrews, explain that if they will "flip" back a few more pages, they will be in Philippians.

Ask the children to find and read together Philippians 4:13. Then put it to rhythm like, "Matthew, Mark, Luke, and John," the game where the children hit their thighs, clap their hands, and snap their fingers with each word.

Now is a good time to let the children stand, stretch, and run in place for thirty seconds. Use a whistle to start and stop this activity.

Then lead them in a quiet worship chorus to prepare for the sermon.

> **PLUG-IN** Trainers should be spread out among the children and be alert to help anyone who is struggling with this exercise.

> If you are concerned because the children are learning the books of the Bible backwards, relax. We'll soon get on track.

> **Spirit Generators** Lead the children in a worship chorus before the Illustrated Sermon. This quiets their spirits and prepares their hearts for the Word of the Lord.

ILLUSTRATED SERMON

Miriam, Leader of the Rhythm Band
(8 minutes)

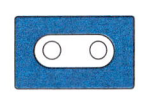

I'd like you to meet Miriam. She has come all the way from the second book of the Bible to see us. Have a Bible open to Exodus 2. **Who knows the name of that book?** Wait for response. **Yes, it's Exodus. Most of us remember her as Moses' big sister. How many of you are big sisters?** Raise your hand to indicate the type of response you want. **Do big sisters have to care for the other children in the family sometimes? Yes. Sometimes they are happy about it, and sometimes not.**

> **Suggestion:** You could prepare a few light gift-wrapped boxes and give them to the trainers secretly. At this time, they could toss them in Miriam's direction.

Tape 📼

MOTHER: Miriam, please hurry and put the pacifier in brother's mouth. You know, if the soldiers hear a baby in here, they'll come looking and . . . well, you know what will happen then.

MIRIAM: Again? I've stuck that thing in there at least ten times in the last two minutes. Why don't we just Super-Glue® it in?

MOTHER: Tries to be patient. Now, now, Miriam, you love little brother as much as we do. Please be a big helper. Hurry now.

MIRIAM: Whines. Pleeease be a big helper. I never get to play outside like my friends do. I always have to stay in here and keep him shushed up. It's, "Miriam, do this. Miriam, do that!" And does he give me any thanks? No. I just end up having to change another dirty diaper, then go wash it out. I wish Mom would switch to Pampers®.

If I told you that Miriam was gifted, would you expect to see a lot of presents come tumbling from the sky upon her? No, not exactly. **Would you expect her to get straight A's on her report card?** Maybe. Maybe not. God did give her some gifts, and she used them wisely.

Let's look at her life. Open the giant book, "The Life of Miriam." Miriam comes to the front, carrying a doll wrapped in a blanket. She sits where all can see her and "cares for her baby" as you talk.

The wicked king of Egypt, Pharaoh, was jealous and worried as he saw so many strong, healthy Hebrews in his land. He tried to kill them off with hard work as slaves, but there seemed to be more and more of them. Would they someday take over his kingdom? This question was always in the back of his mind. He finally resorted to making a decree (or law) that as soon as a Hebrew boy was born, it had to be thrown into the Nile River. So if he couldn't kill off the big, strong men, he would kill the baby boys. What a wimp!

God had a plan for baby Moses to grow up and lead the Israelites out of bondage. But how could he if he was a crocodile's dinner?

Families all over the land cringed when they heard the familiar cries of mothers whose babies were ripped right out of their arms by Pharaoh's soldiers and thrown into the dreaded river to drown or become crocodile food. Could you imagine this? Walk over to Miriam and snatch the doll away and pretend to throw it aside. Miriam cries out in protest. Give it back to her.

God saw a gift in Miriam. She had a talent for loving, and believing and serving that God could use.

Listen closely. Do you think it sounded like this at Miriam's house? Play the *kids POWer hour* tape of a whiny, big sister.

Do you think Miriam acted like that? No. I don't either. Miriam loved her little brother and did everything she could to save him from the Pharaoh.

Moses' mother made a little basket, put Moses in it, and floated it in the river. Miriam, faithful sister, was watching from nearby. Pharaoh's daughter—daughter of the one who ordered the death of such babies—found the basket. Do you suppose Miram thought, "Well, he's crocodile food for sure now"? Again, she showed her courage, a gift from God, and offered to find a Hebrew woman—his own mother, as it turned out—to take care of him for the princess.

That ends chapter one in the story of Moses. Show that you have come to a close on that story in the big book. **Who was the real hero? Moses was delivered from the deadly river because of a gift from his sister—a gift of love and compassion. Miriam had a talent for caring that gave him his start toward the deliverance of their nation.**

Show another chapter entitled "Deliverance on Dry Ground." Turn to the next page while telling the remainder of this story.

Miriam's story did not end in chapter two of Exodus. Chapter fifteen shows her after the great victory of the Israelites marching through the Red Sea—on dry ground! Have "Miriam" leave the baby and pick up a tambourine. As you describe her, she should parade worshipfully around the room, lightly playing her tambourine.

Does it look like she was jealous because she was not the one who led the people to victory? No. She used the talent that God had given her to praise Him. In those times, dancing and singing of sacred songs was done as part of a religious ceremony. The men and women danced at separate times. When the women danced, one woman was the leader and the other women copied her motions. You may want to allow other girls to follow and copy Miriam's motions as she goes around the room.

Close the big book. **Miriam recognized her talents. She knew how she could be a blessing. Each one here has a gift—a talent that the Lord has given you. Let's raise our hands and thank Him for our gift.**

Lighting the Olympic Torch (5 minutes)

Have several older volunteers stand around the room and, beginning at one end, pass a lighted candle from one to the other. The last person should light a large candle at the front of the room.

Reacquaint children with the Olympic torch by using the information given on page 9.

Athletes in the Olympics test their bodies in every way to prove the strength that months and years of practice has earned them. When all the games are over, the flame is extinguished in the closing ceremony.

Invitation and Prayer (5-? minutes)

In Acts chapter two a special fire was lit. Who knows where it came from? Accept such answers as heaven, God, Jesus, etc. **What was it called?** Accept such answers as Holy Ghost, Holy Spirit. **Was this good news spread to other people and lands?** Motion around the room where candle was passed. Wait for "yes" response.

We can receive the gift of the Holy Ghost! This gift is the gift above all other gifts. It gives us power to use the gifts which God has given us. Flex muscles. **Every child is a gifted and talented child. Every child can have the gift of the Holy Ghost.**

The Holy Ghost is a fire that will never go out, no matter how much we are tested. There is no closing ceremony or extinguishing of this flame. Let's invite the Holy Ghost fire into our lives.

Ask children who want to receive the Holy Ghost to come to the front. Ask the trainers and children who have the Holy Ghost to gather around and pray for them. The children who are not praying should join the musician in singing worship choruses.

"God, we thank You for Your promise of the Holy Ghost power and fire. Help us to receive it today and let our lives shine brightly. We are all different, but we know You have a work for each of us. Use us for Your glory. In Jesus' name. Amen."

Review

Line the children up around the room with each standing on a rock to play, "Crossing the Red Sea." As the music plays, they march from rock to rock. When the music stops, ask a review question. If the answer is "yes," all the children on the "no" rocks are out and take their seats. Continue until only one or two are left standing.

At the end of the session, pick up the rocks, remove the Plasti-Tak®, and wipe off the answers. Store in a plastic bag for another time. Answers may be changed to "true" and "false," "agree" and "disagree," or even names, numbers, or letters.

Distribute the *POWer house* papers as the children leave.

Unit Two — In Training

6

Memory Verse: Philippians 4:13

Unit Aim: To help children realize their potential in Christ.

I Can Develop My Gifts

David, Sling Shot Champion

Scripture Text: I Samuel 17:32-37

God gives us gifts, but we must practice to develop them.

Schedule

Date: _____

I. POWer of Worship (25-30 minutes)
  A. Coach's Clipboard (6 minutes)
    • "Practice Makes Perfect" (Scene 1)
    • Announcements
  B. Warm-ups (7 minutes)
    • Request Time
    • Dynamo Specials
    • "Practice Makes Perfect" (Scene II)
  C. Knee Bends (3 minutes)
  D. Exercise: AIM (4 minutes)
  E. Pushups (5 minutes)
    • Missionaries-in-Training

II. POWer of the Word (25-30 minutes)
  A. Training in the Word (5 minutes)
    • Coach/Trainer Dialogue
    • Defining, "citius, altius, fortius"
  B. Biblical Calisthenics (5 minutes)
  C. Spirit Generator (2 minutes)
  D. Illustrated Sermon (7 minutes)
    • Monologue: David, the Sling Shot Champion
  E. Profession N. A. Dither's Demonstration (5 minutes)
  F. Invitation and Prayer (5-? minutes)
  G. Review

On Your Mark

✓ Choose a young man to play the part of David. If one is not available, the coach (whether man or woman) can assume the role by putting on the costume. Give him a copy of the script several days in advance.

✓ The AIMer should zero in on how missionaries "practice" for the field by being missionaries at home. Spotlight one of your PIM's and tell about their experiences before they went to the foreign field. Again, information for this can be obtained in any of the many missionary biographies published by Word Aflame Press. This part of *kids POWer hour* requires some research, but it is well worth the effort. Let's raise up an army of mission-minded Pentecostals with a burden to take "The Whole Gospel to the Whole World."

✓ Add questions to the review notebook.

✓ Check the supply list and gather materials.

✓ Practice the puppet skit, "Practice Makes Perfect." In it a puppet and the coach, standing beside the puppet stage, interact. Ask a musician who plays the instrument used in the script to make a tape of "Jesus Loves Me." A real person could play the role

of the musician. Make a copy of the script and tape it inside the puppet stage for the puppeteer.
- ✓ Acquaint Professor N. A. Dither with the demonstration that he conducts at the end of the Illustrated Sermon. He needs to gather materials.
- ✓ Meet early to have prayer with your staff and discuss any problem areas or plans for improvement.

POWer of Worship

Coach's Clipboard (6 minutes)

Start with the dialogue, "Practice Makes Perfect," (Scene I) between the puppet and the coach. A toy musical instrument is needed.

Practice Makes Perfect

COACH: **We would like to welcome, Marko Grouch, renowned *pianist*.** Substitute name of instrument you are using. **Let's give him a big round of applause.**

MUSICIAN: **Thank you. It's great to be here, Coach. I've heard some pretty POWerful things happen around here!**

COACH: **You're right. That is one reason we have invited you to join us. We would love to hear some of your POWerful music. Before you play, though, could you give us a little background about yourself? We may have some young aspiring musicians here who would like to know what it takes to become as famous as you are.**

MUSICIAN: **I have come a long way since I first struck the keys on my Fisher Price® xylophone.** Appears boastful as he dreamily reminisces. **But I try to stay humble. You know what the Bible says about a "proud look," don't you, Coach?**

COACH: **Uh, yes, I think I do.** Hurries on. **Now, about how you got started playing the** *(names instrument).*

MUSICIAN: Interrupts. **Yes, yes. My mommy and daddy said, "What talent! We'll have to enroll him in music lessons right away."** Adds hastily. **That was after I hit that key on my Fisher Price® xylophone.**

COACH: **Music lessons? That's a good place to start. What age were you when you began lessons?**

MUSICIAN: **Two and a half.** Smiles proudly. **Yes, my teacher said I was the youngest, brightest, cutest, most talented student she ever had. Why, she skipped me right through the first five books straight into that "hard" stuff.**

COACH: **I'm sure she had you practice regularly to turn you into the fine musician you are today.**

MUSICIAN: **Oh yes, yes. Practice—every day.** Reverts to bragging on himself. **She said that with my talent, I could someday play for the President, or even kings or queens. She had never seen so much talent bottled up in one small boy.** Continues to ramble.

COACH: Glances at watch. **We are not kings or queens here, or even the president, but could you favor us with a song before you have to leave?**

MUSICIAN: Suddenly appears to feel inadequate and makes excuses. **Oh, I'm terribly sorry. I left my books at home.**

Supplies

- ❏ *kids POWer hour* tape
- ❏ tape player
- ❏ copies of scripts, *POWer house* papers
- ❏ toy musical instrument
- ❏ puppet
- ❏ tape of instrumental, "Jesus Loves Me"
- ❏ flag of mission country
- ❏ review notebook
- ❏ stop watch
- ❏ biblical costume for David
- ❏ slingshot
- ❏ staff
- ❏ chalkboard and chalk or markerboard and marker
- ❏ pennies
- ❏ vinegar
- ❏ salt
- ❏ tablespoon
- ❏ paper towels
- ❏ jar
- ❏ sign: SOUL FOOD
- ❏ stones from last *POWer hour*'s review game
- ❏ slips of paper
- ❏ hat or basket

COACH: Helpfully. **Don't worry. We have plenty around here.** Hands him a song book. **Go ahead. Wouldn't you like to hear him, boys and girls?** Encourage them to applaud until he accepts.

Musician should try to play a familiar song on the toy instrument, but not be able to figure it out. Coach may turn to other familiar ones and let him try them. Each time he shows considerable struggle and eventually stops.

MUSICIAN: **I'm afraid I'll have to practice a little more on these songs, Coach.**

COACH: Understandingly pats him on the back. **Even a professional like yourself needs to remember the old motto: "Practice makes perfect."**

MUSICIAN: Admits. **Yes, that's right.** Hangs head. **I need to practice more.**

COACH: God gives us gifts, but we must practice to develop them. **Let's give him a hand, boys and girls.** Everyone applauds. **He's going to brush up on these songs and maybe we'll hear from him later.**

As musician leaves everyone calls, "Good bye."

Make announcements. Welcome guests and announce birthdays.

Warm-ups: Sing unto the Lord (7 minutes)

"Just a Little Bit of Faith"
Make this request time. Let the children pick the songs.
Allow a few minutes for Dynamo specials.

At the end of this part of the service, the "musician" slips back in. He announces that he has had time to practice and is ready to play, "Jesus Loves Me." Lead the children in giving a big round of applause as a welcome and another after he has "played" (accompanied by the hidden tape).

Knee Bends: Prayer Time (3 minutes)

Is there something that you wish you could do better? Perhaps play an instrument, or draw a picture, or do math? Encourage the children to respond.

God could give you the ability to play the piano without you taking one lesson. He could give missionaries the ability to suddenly speak the language of the country where they are going. And a few times He has done this, but seldom.

He could have created us so that we were born "knowing everything" so we would never have to go to school. But He didn't. Do you have any idea why? Encourage the children to respond. **Because we need the discipline it requires to study and develop our minds and abilities. It makes us a better person.**

Let's ask God to give us the determination it will take to become better in every area of our Christian lives.

"Heavenly Father, we want to take time today to thank You for Your gifts which You have given to us so freely. Help each of us here to be likewise willing to work—to practice and develop our gifts for Your glory. In Jesus' name. Amen."

Exercise: AIM (4 minutes)

Give the missions report about a missionary's experiences which prepared him to go to the foreign field. Add that country's flag to the wall display.

PERMISSION TO COPY SCRIPT

Pushups: Missionaries-in-Training (5 minutes)

We are talking in this series about winners-in-training. We may have some missionaries-in-training in this group. **If you were going to be a missionary, where would you want to go?** Let children respond.

Did you know that you are a missionary now—a home missionary? You can win souls to Jesus Christ no matter how small you may be. Simply tell people what Jesus has done for you and why you love Him. Invite them to church.

When we prayed did anyone ask God to help you be a better witness—to be able to tell others about Jesus wherever you are? Ask for a show of hands. We all should have our hands up.

What is one way Jesus expects us to try to be a better witness? If an answer does not appear to be coming, ask: **Could it be that we should pray and read the Bible more so we would know what we are talking about?**

Let's practice witnessing. If you were going to tell a friend about Jesus, what would you say? Ask a trainer or two to start this exercise by giving a brief testimony to an "unsaved" friend. Then call for two or three children to volunteer.

POWer of the Word

Training in the Word (5 minutes)

A trainer is sitting on the stage area in front of the children. He is apparently trying to memorize something. He recites, "Citius, altius, fortius," repeatedly. Coach approaches him and asks what he is doing. The trainer responds, "Oh, just trying to remember our memory verse, 'Citius, altius, fortius'."

Coach hesitates, then tells him that he does not think he has the right verse. He asks the children if they think that is the right verse.

Coach continues, "As a matter of fact, 'citius, altius, fortius' is not even a Scripture verse. I think I heard Professor N. A. Dither using that phrase when I walked past his Latin class awhile ago."

The trainer exclaims, "I knew I heard that somewhere! I wish I could remember the memory verse."

Ask the children if they remember the verse, Philippians 4:13. Can they find it in their Bibles, using the biblical calisthenics learned in *kids POWer hour?* After they find it and read it together, review the meaning.

Does this verse mean that I can play the piano without taking lessons or practicing? No. It means I can learn to play the piano if I apply myself because the Lord will bless my efforts. **God gives us gifts, but we must practice to develop them.**

Ask for volunteers to quote Philippians 4:13. Then use the Energy Outlet in the margin.

"Citius, altius, fortius" is an Olympic motto which means "faster, higher, braver," or sometimes "swifter, higher, stronger." In Christ we can go faster and higher, be braver and stronger than we dreamed. We are winners when we remember Philippians 4:13.

Biblical Calisthenics (5 minutes)

Ask children to get their Bibles ready for their biblical calisthenics. Show them how to hold the pages of their Bibles so they can flip from Genesis to

---

This dialogue between the trainer and coach could easily be adapted into a puppet skit with the coach standing outside the stage.

Puppets are great tools to use for teaching memory verses. Children love to teach the verse to the "thick-headed" puppets.

Energy Outlet — Citius, Altius, Fortius

Before defining this phrase for the children, tell them you are going to give them clues to see if they can guess what it means.

Ask everyone to stand and raise their hands as high over their heads as they can. Then ask them to raise their hands higher. Even though they supposedly had raised their hands as high as they could, they will find that they can raise their hands higher—perhaps by standing on tip-toe or stretching their arm muscles.

Next call for a volunteer to run around the room as fast as he can. Unknown to him, time him with a stop watch. When he finishes the lap, give him his time. Then challenge him to do it again, this time "breaking his record." Although he was running "as fast as he could," he will break his record.

What do you think "citius, altius, fortius" means? Let children guess.

"Swifter, higher, stronger." God's Word has an Olympic text: "They that wait upon the Lord shall renew their strength; they shall mount up with wings as eagles; they shall run and not be weary; and they shall walk and not faint" (Isaiah 40:31).

I Samuel. Call out the names of the books as you flip slowly past them. Our Bible story comes from I Samuel 17. Two or three times lead the children through this exercise, having them repeat the names of the books of the Bible after you. Ask them to close their Bibles. How many children can find I Samuel 17 in forty-five seconds? As soon as they find it, they are to jump to their feet. Call out "first, second, third, fourth," etc. as the children stand.

Lead the children in a worship chorus to prepare their hearts for the Word of the Lord.

ILLUSTRATED SERMON

David, Sling Shot Champion (7 minutes)

The Bible story is told as a monologue by David, using the script on page 45.

Professor N. A. Dither's Lesson (5 minutes)

The professor passes out a tarnished penny to each member of the audience. When finished, he shows a shiny new penny in comparison to the children's tarnished ones. He explains that, though both are pennies and are worth the same amount, the shiny one catches our eye.

Using a chalkboard, he writes in large letters, "BRAIN FOOD." He addresses the audience as if they were his class and asks for two volunteers to bring up their pennies. He instructs one to put a small amount of salt on his penny. He instructs the other to put a small amount of vinegar on his penny. Nothing happens.

Then the two volunteers are asked to mix six tablespoons of vinegar and two tablespoons of salt in a jar. They place the dull pennies in the mixture and stir it for a few minutes. Then they rinse the pennies and dry with a paper towel.

What we have seen can be explained scientifically. The professor proceeds with this explanation, being dramatically scientific and drawing on the chalkboard until the whole chalkboard is full. He ad libs as he draws.

The dull film on the pennies forms when oxygen atoms from the air join the copper atoms in the pennies. Shows labels on the items. **Vinegar is acetic acid, and table salt is sodium chloride. When the two are mixed together, they form hydrochloric acid. The dull film on the penny breaks down when the oxygen atoms in it join the atoms in the acid mixture, leaving the penny like new.**

Somewhere near the end of this explanation, the coach holds up a sign, "SOUL FOOD." The professor stops talking in mid-sentence and "freezes."

Invitation and Prayer (5-? minutes)

I think the message from the professor is that no matter who we are here today, we're all "worth" the same to God. He loves us the same. Holds up tarnished penny. **Some of our lives have been "tarnished" like this old penny by the influences—the things and the people**

David, Sling Shot Champion

David enters, dressed in a simple shepherd-type costume, perhaps with sandals on and a sling shot and staff nearby. He is reflecting upon his battle with Goliath, then notices that the children are watching him. He speaks to them.

Oh, hi! Where'd you come from? My name is David and I just came from a battle—not that I like war, you know. But sometimes you "gotta do what you gotta do."

Walks around the room as he speaks. **My main "job" has been to be a shepherd boy—just hanging around and watching sheep. If one tries to run away, I just use the old staff on him.** Reaches out with his staff to one of the children.

At least that's what my seven older brothers think. They think I just lay around and play all day.

Nowadays they have this sibling thing all figured out. If you are the firstborn, you are supposed to act a certain way. If you are the middle child, you are supposed to act another way. And if you are the last born, you are just the "baby" no matter how you look at it. Guess where I am? With seven older brothers? You guessed it! The baby!

Either you seem to do everything right and all the relatives dote on you and spoil you. Or you make a mess of things trying to get some attention.

It's relaxing to lay in the grass and feel the gentle wind blow as the sheep are grazing. I spend a lot of time playing my harp and singing. Then I practice using my sling shot. God gives us gifts, but we must practice to develop them.

One good thing about being the baby is not having to worry about going off to war like my brothers do—at least, that's what I used to think.

I never could understand why people had to fight and kill each other. But one day when a lion, and then a bear, tried to steal one of my lambs, I began to understand things in the big people's world. If there's something you love, like I do my sheep, you may have to fight an enemy to protect what you love and know is right. The lion and bear are history now. Nods head and seems satisfied.

I guess it was that victory over the lion and the bear that gave me courage when I had to take food to the boys who were fighting the Philistines. I could hardly stand hearing Goliath, though a giant he was, defy the armies of God.

What do they say—"It made my blood boil"? You can tease me for being the baby, or you can try to steal my sheep. If you do though—you lose. Smiles. **But don't mess with my God!** Coach and trainers should agree with an "amen."

I said, don't mess with my God! Again, coach and trainers agree with an "amen." **He's an awesome God!**

I didn't need Saul's armor and spear. They weren't my size anyway. Remember, I'm the baby. All the "big boys," however were shaking in their shoes about that time.

What's that song again? Sings. "Faith, Faith, Faith, Just a Little Bit of Faith."

Looks from ceiling to floor. **I sized up that fellow, took one look at my trusty sling shot, and knew I didn't have time for target practice then.** Begins to swing the sling shot around as if ready to "fire" it.

God had been developing faith in me through the ordeal with the lion and the bear. Now was my one and only chance to use it. I'd passed my target practice and this was the real thing! Appears to fire the sling shot.

Pow! One stone was all it took to bring that giant down! Someone asked me why I had five stones. Wasn't I sure I could do it on the first shot? With God's help, I knew I could do it! But, Goliath had four brothers—just as mean and ugly as himself. I was prepared to take care of them as well.

Smiles to self. Runs finger across neck. **I decapitated him, and now his head is my trophy.**

Do you know what my nickname is now? "David, the Sling Shot Champion!" Around town they say, "He's the only one who knows how to get a-head." Smiles.

And with God on our side, we can all get ahead! We are all champions!
Exits.

PERMISSION TO COPY SCRIPT

around us—which draw us away from God. The older we are before we come to God, the more tarnished we become.

Coach may elaborate on specific influences, if necessary.

How many would like to be like the shiny penny? Show one and ask for a show of hands. **Let's ask God to do a "clean-up job" on us. Just the salt alone will not do it. Repentance alone is not enough. Just the vinegar alone—baptism in Jesus' name—will not do it.**

We need to combine these two: repentance and baptism in Jesus' name, and we'll see results. We will become a new creature and "shine" with the Holy Ghost.

Let's ask God to help us develop our lives so they will be pleasing to Him.

Call for all children, both those who have the Holy Ghost and those who do not, to the front to pray.

Review

Use any extra time to practice biblical calisthenics. Have a sword drill, using references from past *kids POWer hours*.

Or play a revision of last *POWer hour's* review game. With a marker, number the stones and place them on the floor around the room in hodgepodge order. On slips of paper write numbers corresponding to the stones and place in a box or hat. As the music plays, the children march. When the music stops, draw a number. The child standing on that number stone is asked a review question. If he answers correctly, he stays in the game. If he misses, he is out.

Distribute the *POWer house* papers as the children leave.

Additional photos from LaMarque, Texas *(continued from page 8)*.

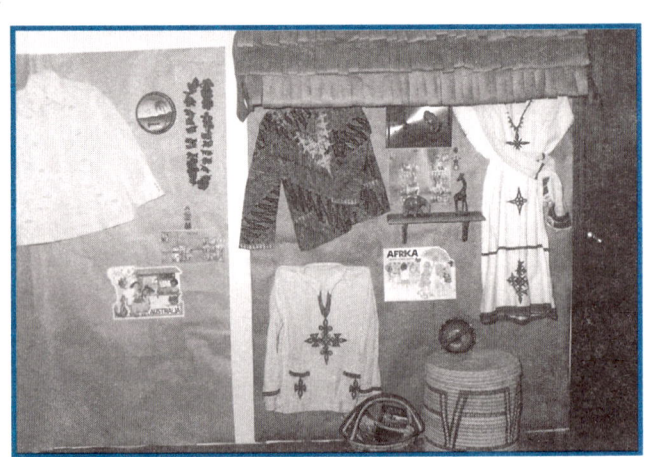

Schedule

Date: _____

I. POWer of Worship (25-30 minutes)
   A. Coach's Clipboard (6 minutes)
      • Announcements
      • Quickie Quiz
   B. Warm-ups (8 minutes)
      • Sing unto the Lord
      • Dynamo Specials
   C. Knee Bends: (3 minutes)
   D. Exercise: AIM (5 minutes)
      • Missionary story
      • Offering
   E. Pushups (3 minutes)
      • Testimony Time
II. POWer of the Word (25-30 minutes)
   A. Biblical Calisthenics (4 minutes)
   B. Training in the Word (10 minutes)
      • Relay Race
   C. Spirit Generator (2 minutes)
   D. Illustrated Sermon (6 minutes)
      • Naaman's Maid, a POWer Witness
   E. Professor N. A. Dither's Lesson (5 minutes)
      • Getting a Charge
   F. Invitation and Prayer (5-? minutes)
   F. Review

On Your Mark

✓ Witnessing is the work of missions. The AIMer's report should be the story of someone being won to Christ because of the witness of a missionary or a native Christian. Again missionary biographies are the resource needed. This story should be told in an exciting, dramatic manner—no stumbling, monotone reading allowed. Missions is exciting! Make it live for your children. Add a flag of the country named in the story to the wall display.

✓ Give a copy of the script of the Illustrated Sermon to the young lady chosen to pantomime the role of Naaman's maid. She should read it through a few times. Then before church go through it with her a couple of times using the *kids POWer hour* tape.

✓ Children are to divide into teams of four for a relay race. If possible, take them outside. Mark off the parking lot or church lawn, using chalk or a sharp stick to mark horizontal lines across the "track." For an inside race, use masking tape. For a large group or indoor race, limit the race to two teams. Place team members vertically on lines 1-4, one team member per line, as shown on the graph on page 49.

✓ Professor N. A. Dither needs to gather his supplies and practice his demonstration beforehand. He

---

Unit Two   In Training

7

Memory Verse: Philippians 4:13

Unit Aim: To help children realize their potential in Christ.

I Can Witness

Naaman's Maid, a POWer Witness

Scripture Text: II Kings 5; Revelation 12:11

No matter what our circumstances we can be a powerful witness for the Lord.

Supplies

- ☐ *kids POWer hour* tape
- ☐ tape player
- ☐ review notebook
- ☐ wrapped candies
- ☐ mission flag
- ☐ timer
- ☐ copy of Illustrated Sermon
- ☐ diary
- ☐ writing pen
- ☐ balloon
- ☐ string
- ☐ flashlights, one for each six children
- ☐ masking tape, sidewalk chalk, or sharp stick for marking racing lines
- ☐ review questions on slips of paper
- ☐ small basket or box
- ☐ POWer house papers

PLUG-IN: In an article in a national magazine, a well-known agnostic told how she was won to Christ by the love and testimony of a seven-year-old girl. Sometimes people who will not listen to another adult will listen to a child.

PLUG-IN: Although a suggestion is given for a special prayer time, always make time to pray for the children's special requests.

Review the mission cheer found on the *kids POWer hour* tape, which you learned in Unit One. It is also on page 128.

should also be prepared to "ramble" a bit as he teaches—true to his character.
✓ Make copies of the *POWer house* paper and the Illustrated Sermon.

POWer of Worship

Coach's Clipboard (6 minutes)

Make announcements. Welcome guests and acknowledge birthdays.

Have a quickie quiz, using questions from your review notebook. The first child to correctly answer a question gets a piece of wrapped candy and is out of the game, giving more children an opportunity to win. If you have a large number of children, you could direct each question to a specific group, *e.g.*, six-year-olds, fourth row, blondes.

Warm-ups: Sing unto the Lord
(8 minutes)

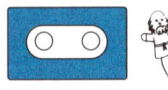

A puppet and the *kids POWer hour* tape should be used to teach this rhyme to the children.

> **Leprosy, leprosy,**
> **This disease didn't stop the King's Captain, you see.**
> **He got victory, victory,**
> **Naaman the leper got victory.**
> **Witnessing, witnessing,**
> **A leper was cured by some witnessing.**
> **Victory, victory,**
> **Even you too, can have victory.**
> **Begin witnessing, witnessing,**
> **Sinners can be saved by some witnessing.**

Use remaining time to sing the children's favorites and have a Dynamo special.

Knee Bends: Soul Winners (3 minutes)

No matter what our circumstances, or our age, we can be a powerful witness for the Lord. Ask children to bow their heads and close their eyes.

Ask God to bring to your mind someone that you see and talk to often, like a neighbor, or a schoolmate, or a store clerk. Give the children a few seconds to think. **Do you have someone in mind? Have you ever prayed for this person? Does this person know God? Could you bear to see them lost forever and know that if you had witnessed to them one time they might have been saved? Sometimes, the person we least expect to receive the message of God's love is the one who needs it the most. Pray with me and ask God to help you love and win this person.**

Exercise: AIM (5 minutes)

Tell an exciting story of a conversion of someone by a missionary or native Christian. Have prayer for your church's PIM's. Add a flag of the country mentioned in the story.

Take the missions offering. Announce the total received to date and remind children of the special project.

Pushups: Testimony Time (3 minutes)

Have "finish the sentence" testimonies. Begin with something like, "I know God can answer prayer because . . . ." Set a timer and announce that in two minutes and twenty-two seconds testimonies stop, even if it is in the middle of a testimony.

POWer of the Word

Biblical Calisthenics (4 minutes)

Repeat these calisthenics to find Philippians 4:13. Use your Bible to show the children how. **Start in the back of the Bible to find Hebrews. Flip slowly past the names of Jesus' disciples, John, Peter, and James. When you reach "James," slow down. Hebrews is right before James. Then continue flipping toward the front, slowly. It is not far to Philippians. Let's read together Philippians 4:13.**

Close your Bibles. Our next assignment is to find today's Bible story. Last *kids POWer hour* we found the story of David and Goliath in I Samuel. Call for a volunteer to come to the front and lead the children through their calisthenics to find I Samuel. When he has done so, give him a round of applause.

Hold your Bible open to I Samuel. Today's Bible story is found in II Kings. You are so close to it your fingers should be warm. Slowly flip toward the back—past II Samuel, I Kings—here we are at II Kings. Can you find chapter 5? When you have found it, raise your hand.

Training in the Word (10 minutes)

Set up the relay track as directed under On Your Mark. If the race is run inside, limit it to two teams. To allow more children to participate, run several races.

Before starting the race, have the children quote the memory passage, Philippians 4:13, several times.

Running with a torch started centuries ago in ancient Corinth. Competitors in the relay race lined up side by side on the starting line. Each runner carried a torch. When the signal was given, they ran to the second line, where another line of runners waited. The first runner on a team handed the torch to the second runner on his team who ran to the next line and passed the torch to the third runner.

From this race came a slogan, "Let those who have the light pass it on."

The Word of God is our light. It shows us how to live a Christian life. We are going to run a race and pass on our light, the Word of God.

Each runner on the starting line must have a Bible in hand. When the signal is given, the runners on the starting line run to the next line. They quote Philippians 4:13 to the second runner, and hand him the Bible. The race continues until the runner crosses the finish line—at which time, he shouts the memory passage. The race is finished when the last runner on the last

team	1	2	3	4
start	1a	2a	3a	4a
	1b	2b	3b	4b
	1c	2c	3c	4c
	1d	2d	3d	4d
finishing line				

> After the exciting relay race, lead the children in a worship chorus to quiet their spirits and prepare them to listen.

team crosses the line. All runners should join hands, raise their arms, and shout together, "We're winners!"

ILLUSTRATED SERMON

Naaman's Maid, a POWer Witness (6 minutes)

As the *kids POWer hour* tape plays, "Naaman's Maid" sits at a table and writes in her diary, pantomiming emotions and actions. Script is on page 51. If you do not have a tape, the script may be copied, hidden in a diary, and the monologue given live.

Professor N. A. Dither's Lesson: Getting a Charge (5 minutes)

Objective: To show that an object with a static electric charge acts like a magnet.

Explanation: Rubbing a balloon on your hair causes the balloon to become negatively charged. You are left with a positive charge. When you move your hand in front of the balloon, you will see the strong attraction between the positive charge and the negative charge.

Procedure: Inflate a balloon. Tie a knot and put a string on it. Tape the string to a table. Rub the balloon on your head to charge it. Hold your hand near the balloon but do not touch it. Watch what happens.

Variation: Rub the balloon on your sleeve and stick it to the wall or make a student's hair stand on end. This experiment works best in low humidity.

Problem: What will happen to a charged balloon when you move your hand in front of it?

Bible truth: **When we are full of God's Spirit, we will act "charged up" and attract sinners to Jesus.**

> As Professor N. A. Dither conducts this demonstration, he should act true to character and start rambling about one of his students or classes and forget what he is doing. At that time, the children will "remind" him. This will reinforce the truth being taught, as well as add interest to the experiment.

Invitation and Prayer (5-? minutes)

How many of you feel so "charged-up" with God's Spirit that you can attract other boys and girls to Him? Let's ask God to "charge us up" so we'll be POWerful witnesses and soul winners for Him.

Have the children form a prayer circle (or circles). **Repeat this echo prayer after me, calling the name of the person on your left.**

Thank You, God, for the power of Your Spirit. Thank You for freedom in this country to freely use this power to be a witness for You. We ask now that You would give *(name the person on your left)* the power to be a witness for You. In Jesus' name. Amen.

You may wish to repeat this prayer and call the person's name on your right.

The Bible says that whenever two or three agree together, whatever they ask shall be done. We have agreed and expect God to answer. All we have to do is go out there and be POWer witnesses.

Review

Write review questions on slips of paper and place in a basket. As the music plays, the children march around the room. When the music stops, the child closest to the basket draws out a review question. If he misses the question, he is out.

If most of your children are readers, use this time for a Bible drill.

Give out the *POWer house* papers as the children leave.

Naaman's Maid, a POWer Witness

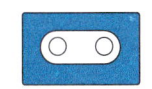

Musical introduction.

Dear Diary: Today is . . . hesitates and sobs . . . **today is a horrible day! Oh, Jehovah, forgive me, please. Today is probably Tuesday, but it is indeed horrible for me. So horrible I can't quite think clearly.**

Yes, it must be Tuesday, for only a couple of sunsets ago my family was together, talking about how good our God is to His people.

Then . . . hesitates again . . . **they came and changed everything—the big, burly Syrian soldiers. I can still hear the cries of my baby sister** . . . **screaming as they tore her out of my mother's loving arms. "Mama! Mama!" was all she knew how to say. But her face said much more. Her eyes were pierced with fear, not understanding why Mama couldn't keep those mean men away.**

I'm sure my voice shrieked as loudly and shrilly as hers, "Mama! Mama!" but I knew we would never see Mama again. Oh, Mama, Mama . . . voice trails off as if she is going to sleep. **If I could only see Mama. . . .**

Musical interlude.

Dear Dairy: Today is Wednesday. I must have cried myself to sleep last evening—cried quietly, though, so as not to anger my new master, Naaman and his wife. At least, diary, I have you. Pantomimes clutching a small group of papers to herself. **Were it not that I had strapped you to my middle before the raid I would be here in Damascus without you. All I have left to remind me of home is you, dear diary.**

The cruel soldiers spoil and do not care. Seems to start to be bitter, but realizes that is not the way to feel, and softens. **Does anyone care? Where is God's goodness? I am a little slave girl now. I can't feel the love of my family so far away from home.**

Oh, Jehovah, my heart should not be so cruel! My lips should not betray You! Your goodness must be all around me. I'll just have to look harder for it in this strange place. I'm sure the One who created heaven and earth can also dwell here in the Captain of the Syrian host's home. Yes, I'll just have to open my eyes and look for God's goodness. Fades out. **I'm looking . . . looking . . . looking.**

Musical interlude.

Dear Diary: Excitedly. **I've found it! Yes! I have a kind mistress. She takes good care of me so I can serve her well. God's goodness is with me! She talks mother-daughter kinds of things with me once in a while. I love to comb her long, beautiful, dark hair.**

She actually wants me to tell her stories of where I came from. I can feel the past come to life again as I tell about how my family prayed together—how we believed together—how we laughed and loved together. Strange it is, but though she is a kind lady, and her husband has received many honors, Mrs. Naaman doesn't laugh a lot. She seems to carry a heavy feeling. I wonder if something is worrying her.

Musical interlude.

Dear Diary: Thank Jehovah that I am a servant girl to Mrs. Namaan! Giggles. **You would not believe your ears, dear diary, if you were human and had ears. I'm actually thankful to be here now.**

Mrs. Naaman needed me to tell her about God, His prophets, and His healing power. I found out that Captain Naaman has leprosy. Only by God's power can a body be rid of that dreadful disease. I wouldn't wish that awful plague on even . . . hesitates . . . **on even the meanest and ugliest of those Syrian soldiers. God has given me a love . . . a miraculous love . . . when I could have a cruel, hurting heart!**

Musical interlude.

Dear Diary: I have been in Captain Naaman's household for some time now. We just received word that he has been cured of his leprosy! Not one, not two, not even three, four, five, or six dips in the yucky Jordan River could heal Captain Naaman. But when he obeyed the prophet Elisha's word and dipped seven times, he was healed! Now his skin is as a newborn baby's skin, pure white and smooth. Thinks reflectively. Hesitates and voice breaks. **A baby's skin—my baby sister—my Mama . . . they would be proud of me.**

She pulls herself together. **No matter where I am, God is good, and I intend to spread the word! No matter what our circumstances, we can be a powerful witness for the Lord.**

Mama? Sister? God is good, isn't He? I love you both. And God, I love You, too—forever.

Finale.

PERMISSION TO COPY

Unit Two — In Training

8

Memory Verse: Philippians 4:13

Unit Aim: To help children realize their potential in Christ.

I CAN SERVE

Elisha, a Prophet's Shadow

Scripture Text: I Kings 19:19-21; II Kings 2:1-15; Matthew 25:21, 23

Before we can be served, we must learn to serve.

Schedule

Date: _____

I. POWer of Worship (25-30 minutes)
  A. Coach's Clipboard (6 minutes)
    • Professor N. A. Dither's Class
    • Announcements
  B. Warm-ups (7 minutes)
    • Praise Choruses
    • Dynamo Specials
  C. Knee Bends (4 minutes)
    • Pray One for Another
  D. Exercise: AIM (5 minutes)
    • Missions Story
    • Offering
  E. Pushups (5 minutes)
    • Lifting Up a Servant
II. POWer of the Word (25-30 minutes)
  A. Biblical Calisthenics (4 minutes)
  B. Training in the Word (4 minutes)
  C. Spirit Generator (2 minutes)
  D. Illustrated Sermon (12 minutes)
    • Bible Reading: II Kings 2
    • Skit: A Mysterious Disappearance
  E. Invitation and Prayer (5-? minutes)
  F. Review
    • My Shadow
    • Charades

On Your Mark

✓ The AIMer's report should focus on the service aspect of missions. If possible, relate a story of a missionary serving someone in a practical way. A missionary's lot is hard work and little glory. Missionary biographies are filled with service anecdotes. Add another flag to the wall display.

✓ Select four trainers or older children to be the "students" in the introductory skit, "Professor N. A. Dither's Class." Give each a copy of the script and have a practice session. Set up an area in front of the room for the professor's class. Students sit with their backs to the children. Provide pencils and paper for students.

✓ Make bright flashcards, "S, E, R, V, E." Staple each to a wooden ruler or rod. These will be used as flashcards by the puppets (or children) to teach a song.

✓ Set up the headquarters for the Missing Persons Bureau as instructed in the script on page 57. Three adults or older teens are needed to be the clerk, the sergeant, and the voice of Elisha. Copies of the scripts can be hidden on clipboards and/or taped to a stack of computer paper. A practice session is needed.

✓ Testimony time calls for giving honor to someone in your church who serves with little recognition. Choose this person in advance. Make a giant thank you card by taping two sheets of posterboard together with wide clear tape. Ask an artistic trainer to decorate the front with an appropriate design and caption. Leave the inside blank for the children to sign.
✓ Add questions to your review notebook. Are you keeping up with data—addresses, telephone numbers, birthdays—on new children? Add comments which will serve as prayer reminders, *e.g.,* family needs, sickness, school or discipline problems.
✓ On slips of paper write names of people studied in this series for a review game of charades.

Supplies

- ❏ *kids POWer hour* tape
- ❏ tape player
- ❏ *POWer house* papers
- ❏ review notebook
- ❏ clipboards
- ❏ sidewalk chalk
- ❏ chalkboard and chalk or markerboard and marker
- ❏ pencils and paper
- ❏ copies of script, "Professor N. A. Dither's Class" and the Illustrated Sermon
- ❏ puppets
- ❏ flashcards: S, E, R, V, E
- ❏ rulers or dowel rods
- ❏ flag of foreign country
- ❏ two sheets of posterboard
- ❏ wide clear tape
- ❏ bright markers
- ❏ computer (optional)
- ❏ continuous feed computer paper
- ❏ telephone (with sound effect, if possible)
- ❏ slips of paper

POWer of Worship

Coach's Clipboard (6 minutes)

Begin the session with the following skit.

Skit: Professor N. A. Dither's Class

Enter Professor N. A. Dither. He appears flustered. His clipboard is upside down with papers flying free, and he has a piece of sidewalk chalk behind his ear. He gives a throw-together appearance. He begins by calling roll, getting the students' names confused.

He then commences his lecture on what it takes to become a teacher. The "class" consists of several trainers (or older children) who sit facing him with their backs to the audience. As students speak, the rest of the "class" and the professor "freeze" until the student sits down, and the lecture resumes.

PROFESSOR: **You are in this class because you want to become teachers, correct?** Students nod their heads. **Today I want to give you some food for thought as you train to become a teacher. Take notes, please. We may have a test over these areas.** Students groan. Professor uses chalkboard to outline his points. Students get pens and paper ready to take notes.

STUDENT #1: Stands and turns to face the children. **Tests? I'm tired of taking tests! I can't wait to be the one who gives the tests. Teachers have the easiest jobs!** Sits down.

PROFESSOR: Writes first point on the board as he talks. **Number 1: Education. Once you have gone to college for four years and have landed a job, you will be expected to keep up on the latest ideas by going back to school in the summer.**

STUDENT #2: Stands up, faces the audience. **Wow! I guess before you can teach, you must be taught. I thought once I was finished here, I wouldn't ever have to study again! That sounds like more homework and more tests! Ugh!** Sits down.

PROFESSOR: Writes point two on board. **Number Two: Time. You will spend a great deal of time doing such things as preparing lessons and tests, and even more time grading papers. Many hours will be spent averaging grades** for report cards, then thinking of nice things to comment about the students to their parents.

STUDENT #3: Stands up, faces audience. **Wow! I thought teachers just sat behind a desk for seven hours a day, barking orders, and a computer graded the work for them!** Sits down.

PROFESSOR: Write on board. **Number 3: Stress. You will have students whom you want to keep happy—like I keep you happy.** Students look at each other in disbelief and snicker. **Then there will be parents, principals, superintendents, and school boards to please as well. You know the old saying, "You can't please all of the people all of the time." That can be stressful. A parent may come in and yell at you if "Little Johnny" or "Little Susie" does not get straight A's. Can you handle that?**

STUDENT #4: Stands and faces children. **Wow! I thought kids were the only ones who got yelled at.** Admits reluctantly. **Teachers have a lot to put up with. Maybe being a kid isn't so bad, after all.**

Students stand and file past the professor, giving him a pat on the back as they return to their seats.

PERMISSION TO COPY SCRIPT

Before we can teach, we must be taught. Before we can be served, we must learn to serve. And that is our *POWer line* for the day. Let's say it together.

Later, we will hear from someone in the Bible who was first a servant, then a leader. He learned to serve, then he was served.

Make announcements. Welcome guests and acknowledge birthdays.

Warm-ups (7 minutes)

Use puppets to teach the new song, "S-E-R-V-E," from the *kids POWer hour* tape.

S-E-R-V-E

Tune: B-I-N-G-O
(1) There is a rule we must obey;
We'll serve Him every day.
S-E-R-V-E, S-E-R-V-E, S-E-R-V-E,
We'll serve Him every day.
(2) There is a rule we must obey;
We'll serve Him when we pray.
S-E-R-V-E, S-E-R-V-E, S-E-R-V-E,
We'll serve Him when we pray.
(3) There is a rule we must obey;
We'll read our Bible each day.
S-E-R-V-E, S-E-R-V-E, S-E-R-V-E,
We'll read our Bible each day.

"The Servant of All"
"I Will Serve Thee Because I Love Thee"

PLUG-IN: If puppets are not available to teach this song, use the letter flashcards as visuals. Give each card to a child. As the song is sung, the child jumps up and holds up their sign, then sits down. When one verse is complete, they have spelled the word three times. For the next verse, they pass their sign to someone near them. This allows more children to participate.

Knee Bends: Pray One for Another (4 minutes)

Not only are we to love and serve one another, we are to pray for one another. One of the best ways we can serve and help others is to pray for them.

Instruct trainers to help the children form prayer rings of three to five children. Allow a few seconds for the children to share with those in their circle any special needs they have.

We are going to pray for everyone in our circle by name. Lead the children in congregational prayer. Close by asking everyone to say, "In Jesus' name. Amen."

> **PLUG-IN** Boys and girls will automatically segregate. Do not make an issue of it. Let them join the group they are comfortable with, even if there are six in the circle. Ask them to hold hands. Again, if there is a problem with this, do not make an issue of it. Trainers should join circles with "gaps" and connect these circles by joining them.

Exercise: AIM (5 minutes)

Tell a story of a missionary who won someone to the Lord by practical service. Point out that one meaning of the word "minister" is "servant."

About this time the children probably need an activity break. Make it a "praise break" to thank the Lord because we know the gospel and can help take it to other lands.

Ask the children to stand and give the Lord a "wave offering." Tell them to put their offering in their hand and double up their fist, so no one but God sees what they have. If they do not have an offering, tell them to put "love" in their fist. Pretend to pull love from your heart and hold it in your fist.

Have everyone repeat after you words or phrases of praise, "I love You, Jesus. I give myself to You. Praise the Lord." Then let them march around and give their offering.

Keep the children posted on the total of the offerings by keeping the graph up-to-date. Isn't it interesting knowing how your money translates into foreign currency?

Pushups: Testimony Time (5 minutes)

The Bible tells us to give honor to those who deserve it. Many who serve in practical ways receive little recognition. Choose one of these "ministers" whom the children know to honor. It could be the janitor, a lady who cooks and serves at church dinners, the church secretary—anyone who serves faithfully, but receives little honor.

What is another word for "minister"? Servant.

Use the testimony time to lift up a "minister" of our church. Point out that not all ministers minister in a pulpit.

Start by asking the children to tell something that the person chosen has done to serve the church. List the things named on the "giant thank you card." Then let the children line up and sign the card, using bright markers.

> **PLUG-IN** You might want to give this person a special invitation to *kids POWer hour*. If he or she is present, inform trainers what is going to happen. Ask them to be prepared to start the testimony time by telling something this person has done for the church or for them personally. If the honoree is not present, choose a committee of children to deliver the card.

> Instructions for making the giant thank you card are under On Your Mark.

POWer of the Word

Biblical Calisthenics (4 minutes)

Briefly review the biblical calisthenics learned to this point—how to find the Book of Psalms, the Gospels, Hebrews, Philippians, I Samuel, I Kings.

Training in the Word (4 minutes)

Ask the children to use their biblical calisthenics to find Philippians 4:13. Read together. Explain again that "all things" are limited to things that please God. "Through Christ" means with His help and approval.

Make a list of a variety of things, *e.g.*, witness to a teacher, not cheat on a test, eat a large pizza by myself, obey my parents, lift a two hundred pound weight, beat up on the class bully, make friends with a new kid at school. Instruct the children to say together, "I can. . . ." Then from the list, you insert something. If the children agree that they can do that "through Christ" (with His help and approval), they should finish the verse. If they do not think that Christ has promised to help them do the thing named, they remain silent.

Example: Children say, "I can. . . ." Coach inserts, "Eat a large pizza by myself." Children remain silent.

Children say, "I can. . . ." Coach inserts, "Witness to my teacher." Children respond, "Do all things through Christ which strengtheneth me."

> Lead the children in a worship chorus to prepare their hearts for the Word of the Lord.

ILLUSTRATED SERMON

Elisha, a Prophet's Shadow (12 minutes)

The Illustrated Sermon places the Bible story in a modern setting. To help children realize that the story is true, while the setting is fictional, briefly tell of the calling of Elisha to follow Elijah (I Kings 19:19-21). Then have the children follow along in II Kings 2 (using biblical calisthenics to find it) as you tell the story of Elijah's translation. Read aloud verse 1, then relate in your words what happened in verses 2-7. Pick up reading at verse 8 and read through 14, paraphrasing as you go to be sure the children get the picture. Conclude by telling about the sons of the prophets' search for Elijah.

Now you are ready for the skit on page 57.

Invitation and Prayer (5-? minutes)

Musician plays.

What did Elisha ask Elijah to give him? A double portion of his spirit. **And that is what happened. Elisha performed exactly twice as many miracles as Elijah. What if Elisha had not asked for this power? Would he have received it? No. If we want Holy Ghost power, what must we do? Ask for it! Jesus promised that if we would ask, we would receive.**

Ask for heads to be bowed, eyes closed, and a show of hands of those who want the baptism of the Holy Ghost. Invite those who raised their hand to pray. Have trainers ready to pray with them.

Distribute the *POWer house* papers as the children leave.

Review

Just for fun, divide into pairs. Spread out across the room so each pair is separated from the others by a few feet.

First, the older child is the person and the younger is the shadow. Whatever the person does, the shadow must do. When time is called, the younger becomes the person and the older the shadow.

For a review game, play, "Charades." On slips of paper write the names of people studied in this series. Let volunteers draw a name to act out.

Elisha, a Prophet's Shadow

A clerk is sitting at a computer. A telephone is nearby. If no computer is available, the person could be situated so that it seems he is working on a computer. (Children's imaginations are wonderful visuals.)
Phone rings. Clerk answers.

CLERK: **Good morning. Missing Persons Bureau. How may I help you?** Listens. **Yes. Yes. Can you describe the person?** Types as he takes information. **Where was he last seen?** Listens and types again. **What was his occupation? Are there any other people who may have been involved with him and have clues to his whereabouts?** Listens. **Yes. We'll do what we can. Good-bye.** Hangs up phone.
Buzzes intercom (real or imaginary). **Sergeant** *(name)*, **could you come in here, please?**

ENTER SERGEANT.

SERGEANT: **A new case, huh? Bring it up on the screen.** Looks over the clerk's shoulder as they appear to read the information. **Name, Elijah. Profession, prophet. Interesting. Can you pull up any background on this preacher?**
Clerk appears to type.

SERGEANT: Reads. **The name Elijah means, "My God is Jehovah." Born in Gilead, east of the Jordan River. Parents' names are not known. Grew up during the time when people were taking sides between the God of heaven and the gods of the heathen.**

CLERK: **So we know whose side he was on—from the meaning of his name.**

SERGEANT: **Right. These prophets live daring lives. They are not afraid to speak up and say what they believe. They usually are not very wealthy, but it seems like when they say something is going to happen, it happens. And the richest person on earth cannot stop it.**

CLERK: **He was last reported to have been leaving in a chariot of fire during a recent whirlwind.**

SERGEANT: **Get me a listing, if you can, of the things he's claimed to have done. We'll go from there**.
Sergeant leaves the room. Clerk types on computer. Mutters, "Hummm. Amazing! Unbelievable!" Sergeant returns.

SERGEANT: **Let's see what you have.** Picks up stack of continuous computer paper and pretends to read. Script can be taped to papers. **Proclaimed to King Ahab that it would not rain until he said—it came to pass. Was miraculously fed by ravens. Performed a miracle for a widow and her son that provided them with enough food to live on. Later raised the widow's son back to life. Called fire down from heaven by praying a simple prayer which made a believer out of the worshipers of Baal.**

SERGEANT: Flips through pages rapidly. **Page after page of miracles. Amazing! Is there anyone he was connected with that might know something about him?**

CLERK: **Yes, on page 213 there is someone with a similar name—Elisha.**

SERGEANT: Turns pages. **Strange. A name so similar, and a life so similar. It seems he was Elijah's servant. Like a shadow, Elisha went everywhere the old prophet did until his disappearance. Here's a phone number of a school they were involved with. Let's see if we can find any leads there.**
Clerk dials phone. A hidden person with a microphone and a copy of the script speaks the part of the recorded message and Elisha.

MESSAGE: **Thank you for calling EEU—School of the Prophets. If you are calling from a touch-tone phone and wish to speak to registration, please enter a "one" now. If you wish to speak with records office, enter a "two" now. If you wish to speak with financial aids, enter a "three" now. For other information, please hold and an operator will assist you.** Pause. **EEU—School of the Prophets. How may I help you?**

SERGEANT: **This is Sergeant** *(name)* **from the Missing Persons Bureau. We're calling for information about a prophet named Elijah, believed to have disappeared in a whirlwind. Can you help us?**

MESSAGE: **One moment, please. I'll connect you with our new president, Elisha.**

ELISHA: **Hello, Elisha speaking.**

SERGEANT: **This is Sergeant** *(name)* **from the Missing Persons Bureau, and we're seeking information about a prophet named Elijah who has mysteriously vanished.**

ELISHA: **Yes, I knew Elijah well. I was his servant. I was one of the few people who saw him go. He was getting older, and I had been chosen by God to take over his work here with the school and the students of prophecy.**

SERGEANT: **I understand from my reports that not only his disappearance, but his whole life, was one miracle after another. Is that correct?**

ELISHA:	Yes. I followed him very closely, especially after I knew I would be taking his place. I knew that before I could be served, I had to learn to serve. I was his right hand. I served him in every way I could.
He lived up to his name, "My God is Jehovah." He told me to watch him and I did. I knew that the on-the-job training I was receiving was going to end soon so I became his shadow.
SERGEANT:	Did he say anything before he left that gave you a clue as to where he went or if he was coming back?
ELISHA:	Not a clue. He only asked what one thing he could do for me before he left. Of course, I did not know what to say. I thought for a moment and decided I wanted to be able to do all the things he did—and more. So I asked for a double portion of his spirit. He said that if I saw him leave, my wish would be granted.
SERGEANT:	Yes. And you did see him leave, didn't you?
ELISHA:	Yes, I did. A strong, whirling wind came and picked Elijah up in it. Then a chariot, thousands of times more glorious than Ahab's, appeared in a blazing light in the sky. The chariot and the creatures that drew it seemed to be on fire. Elijah stepped into it and was gone.
SERGEANT:	Gone, huh?
ELISHA:	The chariot carried him home—to heaven.
SERGEANT:	Amazing! And now can you do miracles as he did?
ELISHA:	Yes. As I watched, he dropped his mantle, that's the cape he wore. He had used it to smite the river and part the water. I've already tried it. It works for me, too.
SERGEANT:	Uh . . . thank you, Mister Elisha. We're going to study this information and may be calling you for another interview. Uhhh . . . in the meantime, hang on to that mantle. I can't really understand it, but it sounds like Elijah left you a very special gift.
ELISHA:	Yes, sir, I will. Good-bye.
SERGEANT:	**Good-bye**. Hangs up phone thoughtfully.
SERGEANT:	To clerk. **A preacher. Miracles. Another man who shadowed him and served him. A whirlwind and fiery chariot—and a "powerful mantle."** Wait till the big boss hears this one. Somehow, though, I just can't help believing the story.

Sergeant and clerk walk away looking at printout and both shaking their heads.

PERMISSION TO COPY

Plan Ahead

Unit three is heavenly and requires preparation. After all, no one gets to heaven without preparation. Read pages 65-67 for decor suggestions. Decide which ideas will work best for your situation, then recruit lots of help. Scenes need to be painted, gates made, and angels costumes sewed and assembled. Most of the work can be done beforehand and slipped into place after *POWer hour* 9.

Schedule

Date: _____

I. POWer of Worship (25-30 minutes)
  A. Coach's Clipboard (8 minutes)
    • Paralympians Demonstration
    • Announcements
  B. Warm-ups (8 minutes)
    • Puppets
    • Praise Choruses
    • Dynamo Specials
  C. Stumbling Blocks or Stepping Stones? (3 minutes)
  D. Exercise: AIM (4 minutes)
    • Mae Iry's Story
    • Offering
  E. Knee Bends (3 minutes)
    • A Prayer for Missions
  F. Pushups (3 minutes)
II. POWer of the Word (25 -30 minutes)
  A. Training in the Word (5 minutes)
  B. Biblical Calisthenics (5 minutes)
  C. Illustrated Sermon (7 minutes)
    • Moses, a Tongue-Tied Leader
    • Testimony from or about a Disabled Person
  D. Invitation and Prayer (5-? minutes)
  E. Review
    • Paralympics Relay Race

On Your Mark

✓ Gather wheelchairs, crutches, leg braces, etc., for the Paralympics demonstration. Check with church members, neighbors, the senior citizens' center, service organizations, etc., for items to borrow. Display these around the room.
✓ Give a copy of the story of Mae Iry to the AIMer.
✓ Have a short practice session with the puppeteers who are going to present the rhythm rhymes.
✓ Add review questions to your notebook.
✓ The Illustrated Sermon is presented as a skit. Four children are needed. Make copies of the script. Have a short practice session.
✓ Acquaint Professor N. A. Dither with his role in the service, *e.g.,* introducing the Paralympics, receiving the offering.
✓ Is there a disabled person in your church or community who would be willing to talk to the children? If so, ask them to share how they have overcome difficulties. If no one is available, share with the children the story of someone you know or a true story from history. (Check at your public library.)
✓ On slips of paper write ways the children can quote the memory passage. "Whisper." "Shout." "Jog in

Unit Two   In Training

9

Memory Verse: Philippians 4:13

Unit Aim: To help children realize their potential in Christ.

I Can Do My Best

Moses, a Tongue-Tied Leader

Scripture Text: Exodus 4:1-17; Philippians 4:13

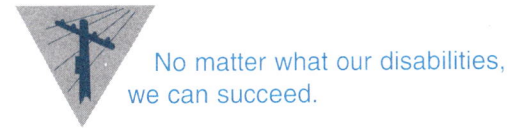

No matter what our disabilities, we can succeed.

Supplies

- ☐ *kids POWer hour* tape
- ☐ tape player
- ☐ wheelchair, crutches, leg braces, etc.
- ☐ review notebook
- ☐ flags from mission display
- ☐ *POWer house* papers
- ☐ several large stones or rocks
- ☐ a copy of Mae Iry's story for AIMer
- ☐ copies of the Illustrated Sermon, optional
- ☐ timer
- ☐ ball
- ☐ slips of paper
- ☐ small box or hat
- ☐ small awards, *e.g.,* pencils, stickers
- ☐ crown
- ☐ robe
- ☐ hand fan
- ☐ serving tray
- ☐ glass of ice water and/or fruit
- ☐ stick
- ☐ masking tape

PLUG-IN Be time conscious with this activity. Every child in your group will want to participate. Tell them that if time permits there will be another Paralympic at the close of the service.

---

place." "Touch your toes." "Turn your back to audience." You will need one slip for each child. Add as much variety as possible. If you run out of ideas, duplicates are acceptable. Place in a box or hat labeled, "How to."

✓ Use masking tape to mark off four or five lines 2'-3' apart for the Paralympic review game.

POWer of Worship

Coach's Clipboard (8 minutes)

Professor N. A. Dither should begin the class by entering on crutches. He shares the following information with the children.

The Olympic Creed says: "The most important thing in the Olympic Games is not to win but to take part, just as the most important thing in life is not the triumph but the struggle. The essential thing is not to have conquered but to have fought well."

The Paralympics are games played about two or three weeks after the regular Olympics. They include athletes who are blind, or visually impaired, paraplegics (whose legs are partially paralyzed), quadriplegics (whose legs and arms are partially or totally paralyzed), people with cerebral palsy, amputees, dwarfs, and those with other disabilities. In some cases, only minor modifications are made to the rules of a sport to accommodate the athlete's disabilities.

Paralympians complete the wheelchair marathon of twenty-six miles in about ninety minutes. This is approximately 3 1/2 minutes per mile. Four miles an hour is a good walking pace. These wheelchair racers are going almost eighteen miles an hour. That's moving right along.

Single leg amputees have high-jumped 6' 8"—only 6" less than the Olympic record. Use a yardstick to measure approximately how high two or three children can jump.

Blind swimmers have come within one one-hundredth of a second of qualifying for the U. S. Olympic team. Have children blink. That's how close they came to making the Olympic team.

Let as many children as time will allow participate in a Paralympics demonstration, using the wheelchairs, crutches, etc. Challenge them to go from one end of the room to another. Have trainers or older children close by to catch anyone who may lose his balance.

Repeat together the *POWer line*. **No matter what our disabilities, we can succeed.**

Warm-ups (8 minutes)

Start by having the puppets teach the children this rhythm rhyme.

Group 1:	**Don't quit.**
Group 2:	**For the devil is looking.**
Group 1:	**Don't quit.**
Group 2:	**The devil wants you to sin.**
Group 1:	**Don't quit**
Group 2:	**Living for Jesus**
ALL:	**For He is coming back again—real soon!**

Here is another song/chant for the puppets to teach the children. Sing/chant the first line with the pitch going up slightly at the end. Sing/chant the second line with the pitch going down slightly at the end. Going up on the third line, and down on the fourth.

Never, never, never, never, never give up.
Never, never, never, never, never give in.
Never, never, never doubt the Word of God
For that would be a sin.

Spend several minutes in praise choruses.
"God Can Do Anything But Fail"
"We Are Standing on Holy Ground"

Stumbling Blocks or Stepping Stones? (3 minutes)

Place several large stones in a path on the floor in front of the class. Demonstrate how they can be stumbling blocks or stepping stones. Let several children walk on them. Discuss how disabilities can be stumbling blocks or stepping stones.

Exercise: AIM (4 minutes)

Mae Iry was a widow with a limited education and four children, who cleaned offices in Chicago in the early 1900's. Polio had left the right half of her face paralyzed. She spoke and ate with the mobile left half of her mouth and charmed everyone with an infectious one-sided grin. She may have looked like a poor, crippled, uneducated, single mom to many people, but there was something special about Mae Iry. She had a call of God on her life.

God had called Mae to be a missionary to China. When her children were grown, she, her daughter and son-in-law crossed the ocean to carry the gospel.

Something miraculous happened in China which has happened to few missionaries. The Chinese language is extremely difficult to learn and Mae despaired of ever learning it. She could barely make herself understand between services. But, when she began to preach, the Holy Ghost touched her twisted mouth and she gave out the Word in fluent Chinese.

She had been in China for many years when war broke out. When the Japanese invaded their city, Mae led the city leaders in prayer. After praying, she advised them to meet the enemy with gifts and food. The Chinese did and their lives were spared.

Later the Chinese begged Mae to round up the girls and young women and take them to the mission where they would be safe. The enemy had every right to keep her from doing this, but she went from house to house rescuing the girls. She said, "Jesus gave me favor. The officers helped me, showing the courtesy they reserved for the aged." She added, "My crooked mouth probably helped, too."

Mae Iry, widowed, poorly-educated, disabled, was used by God. Her disabilities became stepping stones which helped her bring many souls to Christ.

No matter what our disabilities, we can succeed.

Professor N. A. Dither could take the offering. In keeping with his name, he might want to take "two" offerings. It could be surprising what he receives the second time.

> This story is condensed from Profiles of Pentecostal Missionaries, compiled by Mary H. Wallace, published by Word Aflame Press.

Keep the children informed on the offering total for the special missions project.

Knee Bends (3 minutes)

Divide into prayer circles. Take down the flag of mission countries from the wall display. Give each circle a flag. Instruct them to go around the circle saying sentence prayers, praying for the missionaries and the children in the country their flag represents. If flags are not available, let each circle choose a country to pray for.

Pushups (3 minutes)

Tell the children that testimony time is devoted to giving thanks for our health. "I'm thankful that I can see the pretty flowers God has made." "I'm thankful I can hear someone singing a lovely song." "I'm thankful my legs can run fast."

Set the timer for two minutes and eight seconds. Toss a ball to a child. He tells one thing he is thankful for then throws the ball to another child. Encourage the children to keep the ball rolling by throwing it to someone who has not testified. If the group is small, let the children testify more than once to take up the allotted time.

POWer of the Word

Training in the Word (5 minutes)

Let the children who can quote Philippians 4:13 line up. They draw a slip from the "how to" box/hat. They should stand behind the podium and use the mike to say this verse. Give each child who does so a small award. Allow children who "catch on" after the verse has been quoted several times to join the line.

Biblical Calisthenics (5 minutes)

Find in your Bible the book which answers these questions. When you find the answer, jump to your feet, but zip your lip until four people are standing. Then everyone standing can shout out the answer together.

What is the first book of the Bible?

What book contains many songs written by David?

Where is the memory passage just quoted?

Name one of the four Gospels.

What is the last book of the Bible?

What book in the Bible tells about the Day of Pentecost?

What is the first book of the New Testament?

What is the last book of the Old Testament?

PLUG-IN: If the majority of the children are struggling to find any of these answers, show them how to find the book needed. Trainers should be seated among the children ready to help preschoolers or slow readers. Everyone needs to be able to jump up sometime, even if they have to be helped to do it.

ILLUSTRATED SERMON

Moses, a Tongue-Tied Leader (7 minutes)

The children chosen in advance present the pantomime, using the script from page 64.

> **PLUG-IN:** Moses talked with a speech impediment. If there are children with speech impediments in your children's church, "Moses" may choose to use a normal voice. If an impediment is used, make sure it draws compassion from the children and not mockery.

• ▶

Invitation and Prayer (5-? minutes)

No matter what our disabilities, we can succeed.

In some way we are all disabled. One may have a learning disability and have trouble reading. Another may have a speech disability and have trouble talking. Another may have a mechanical disability and not be able to do much more than push a button or flip a switch. Another may have an artistic disability and not even be able to draw a straight stick man. Everyone is disabled in some way.

But what does Philippians 4:13 say? Quote together. **I may not be able to operate a computer, but I can succeed in some way. You may have a learning disability, but be able to repair a complex machine or build a bird house or draw a lovely picture.**

With Jesus' help we can do whatever He asks us to do. When Jason's dad asked him to paint the lawn furniture, Jason said, "But, Dad, I can't. I don't have any paint or a brush." What do you think Jason's dad did? Sure. He gave Jason the materials needed to do the job.

When Jesus asks us to do something for Him, He gives us the tools—the courage, the ability—to do the job. Remember Mae Iry? She did not have money or education or even a perfect body, but God gave her the strength to go to a foreign land and work for Him.

Would you like to consecrate your abilities and disabilities to Jesus today? If so, come to the front and we will pray together.

Lead the children in an echo prayer of consecration.

"Lord Jesus, I love You and want to serve You. I give to You my abilities—everything I can do—and my disabilities—everything I cannot do. Use me in any way You choose. I am Your child. In Jesus' name. Amen."

As children keep their heads bowed and their eyes closed, lead them in a song of consecration such as, "I'm Yours, Lord."

Review

If time allows, have a Paralympic review quiz. Line up as many children as you have wheelchairs, crutches, etc. Give each child a device. Go down the line asking review questions. When a child answers correctly, he moves forward to the next line. When he reaches the finish line, he is declared a winner, given a round of applause, and out of the game. He gives his aid to another child who starts on the first line.

Give each child a *POWer house* paper as he leaves.

> **PLUG-IN — Coming Soon**
>
> Have major plans for Unit Three already been made? It is time to start turning the gym into heaven's gate.
>
> A staff meeting is essential at the beginning of each unit. Organization saves confusion and it can save souls.
>
> A well-planned *POWer hour* is free from confusion and creates an atmosphere conducive for the moving of God's Spirit.

Moses, a Tongue-Tied Leader

As prince of Egypt, Moses, wearing a crown and robe, is surrounded by several servants fussing over him and running to do whatever he asks. One is fanning him, another carries a serving tray containing ice water or fruit. A musician plays background music, fitting the mood and action. The "narrator" and "voice" is hidden, using a microphone. One person could read both parts, but should use a different tone for each.

SERVANT 1: Flatteringly. **Prince Moses, you are looking more handsome and stronger every day.**

SERVANT 2: **Yes, Prince Moses, someday you will become ruler of Egypt. What a magnificent king you will be.**

SERVANT 3: **Only the best teachers in the land have tutored you. You are surely the smartest young man in the land.**

Moses appears to love every minute of this attending. He takes a piece of fruit or glass of water from the tray. Then with a flip of his hands, he sends them away. He stares into the distance and talks to himself as he drinks or snacks.

MOSES: **There is a little voice inside me. It keeps telling me that I am going to be a great leader. But something also tells me it may not happen right away. I have made up my mind to stick to the heritage my mother, Jochebed, taught me. I'll do anything to see that the Hebrews, my people will not suffer much longer under the Egyptian's rule of oppression.** Stands to his feet. Sticks out his chest and declares boastfully. **I have the power and position to arrange just about anything.** Turns his back to the audience and stands frozen as the narrator reads.

NARRATOR: **One day when Moses was walking in the brickyards, he saw an Egyptian overseer beating a Hebrew slave. This made Moses very angry because the Hebrews were his people. He killed the Egyptian, thinking the Hebrews would hail him as their hero. He was mistaken. He had to run for his life because killing one of the king's officers was unpardonable. Too late, he realized he should not have acted so rashly.**

MOSES: Turns to face the audience, removing his crown and cape. **If only I could do it over. I would think before acting.** I blew it! I thought I could deliver my people from Egyptian slavery. But I learned I can do nothing without God's help.

Now who will deliver my people? I am eighty years old, ready to retire. My first forty years I spent learning the ways of the Egyptians.

The last forty I have spent un-learning a lot of things. But it is too late now for me to help my people. Yes, it is too late for me. I'm getting old.

Besides that I can't talk plain. When I try to talk, my tongue gets tangled up and I stutter. I even have trouble understanding myself—when I talk to myself, which is pretty often these days.

No one will listen to me—probably not even God. He may have given up on me, too. Puts head down on hands. He suddenly looks up and sees a burning bush. Points into the distance.

Look, everybody! See the fire—over there by that bush? A bonfire. Maybe there's going to be a consecration service. I could use one.

VOICE: **Moses! Moses!**

MOSES: **Someone must be calling me for supper.**

VOICE: **Moses! Moses!**

MOSES: **We must be roasting hot dogs tonight. It's not like palace food, but I can't expect royal food on a shepherd's salary, can I?** Picks up a stick. **This should make a good wiener roasting stick.** Moves closer in the direction of the "fire." **My, that fire is hot! Hummm, that's strange. Very strange. This bush is on fire, but it is not burning. It looks just like it did before the fire started. Very strange indeed!**

VOICE: **You are on holy ground, Moses. Take off your shoes.**

Moses trembles and hurries to obey. Seems to have trouble removing his shoes because he is so frightened. Then he bows.

MOSES: **W-W-W-hat? God? Is that You, God?** Pauses. **You haven't forgotten me? And you haven't forgotten Your people in Egypt?**

I blew it, God, and I am so sorry. I'm about ready for the boneyard. I'm not young and strong anymore. I can't do anything. Pauses.

Lead the children of Israel out of Egypt? Me? God, You've got the wrong person. There are many more men much more capable than I am. Why, I can't even talk plain.

What? You are the One who made my tongue? You are the One who will go with me?

But, Lord, the people would not trust me after what I did in Egypt. You say, "Trust Me"? Oh, yes, Lord, I will trust You. If You will go with me, I will go. I will go. I will go. Picks up shoes and exits.

PERMISSION TO COPY SCRIPT

Unit Three   **Go for the Gold**

HEAVEN'S HEROES

Memory Passage: I John 5:4

Unit Aim: To show how people in the Bible overcame in situations similar to ones faced by children today.

Room Decor

A Glimpse of Heaven

The atmosphere should be heavenly! The center front looks like a gate to heaven. The gate opens in the center and each *POWer hour* heaven's hero walks through it. This can be done with a white sheet or a cardboard gate. Place white columns on each side of the gate. See the illustrations.

Behind the gate, place a drawing of heaven, enlarged from art on page 125. Glitter or glitter paints can be used to add "sparkle."

Clouds can be made of polyester filler (used in pillows). Just pull a gob from the package and spray lightly with gold paint. Arrange these in front of and at the bottom of the gate—remember we are "above the clouds."

If you have a permanent place for *kids POWer hour* and do not have to share with other departments, hang stars, planets, and clouds from the ceiling. (Fishing line is practically invisible.) Or place them low on the walls. The effect needs to be that the children are among the stars.

Place a sign pointing to heaven on the edge of the platform. The heroes walk up to the sign to tell their story.

A sign over the gate reads, "Heaven's Heroes." Make the letters in gold with glitter.

Glory Avenue

On one wall make "Glory Avenue" with gold foil paper. Reproduce enough of the mansion from page 125 so there is one for each child who has obeyed the plan of salvation, and by faith, one for each child who will obey before the unit is finished.

Give each child who qualifies a "mansion" to place on Glory Avenue. If there is time before the beginning of the session, set up a work table and let the children decorate their mansions with gold paint and glitter.

Theme Songs

The theme song for this unit, "Angels Watchin' Over Me," is on the *kids POWer hour* tape, along with several other songs correlating with the material.

Guardian Angels

Two angels, Alpha and Beta, are the mascots throughout the unit. The children will soon know them by name and personality.

The angels wear white robes with silver or gold halos, circles of wire wrapped with tinsel. Wings would add to the effect. (See illustration below.)

Angels may be male or female, since in heaven they are neither.

Supplies needed by the angels each *POWer hour* are:
- trumpet (toy or real)
- binoculars (toy or real)
- trophy and/or crown
- "The Book of Life" (book or scroll)

These will not be listed on the supply list each week.

The Book of Life may be made from white paper trimmed and lettered in gold. A family Bible with a false cover will work. Or for a scroll use a white piece of paper 3 1/2" by 11". Glue or tape each end to a 4" dowel rod. Roll toward the center and tie with a gold ribbon.

Novelty stores have plastic trophies at reasonable prices. Or a plastic sundae glass can be sprayed gold and glued to a piece of wood.

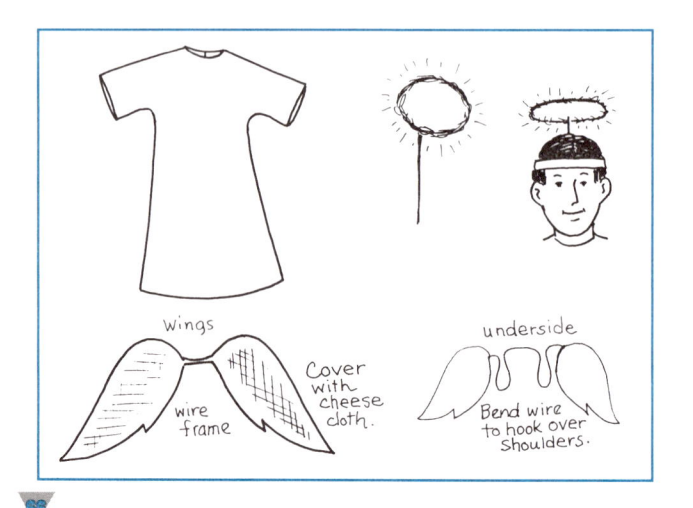

The "coach" used in the last two units is dropped and the leader is simply the "director."

Missions

AIMer's Reports

In this unit short stories are given of missionaries who have received their crown of life.

Offering

Paint a box gold. Make a slit in the top so the money can be dropped in without opening the box. Add jewels. On a standup sign (or on the front of the box), write: *"Lay up for yourselves treasures in heaven" (Matthew 6:20).*

Cover a table or stand with a velvet or lace cloth. Place the box and sign on it. Make this an impressive display.

Giving is an attribute of God and an important part of being a Christian. Selfish people are not "Christlike." Encourage your children, even the youngest ones, to work for money to give to missions. They can ask their parents, grandparents, and older friends for jobs. Ask your pastor to help by keeping parents informed on *kids POWer hour* projects and encouraging them to give their children money for the offering.

Prayer Spinner

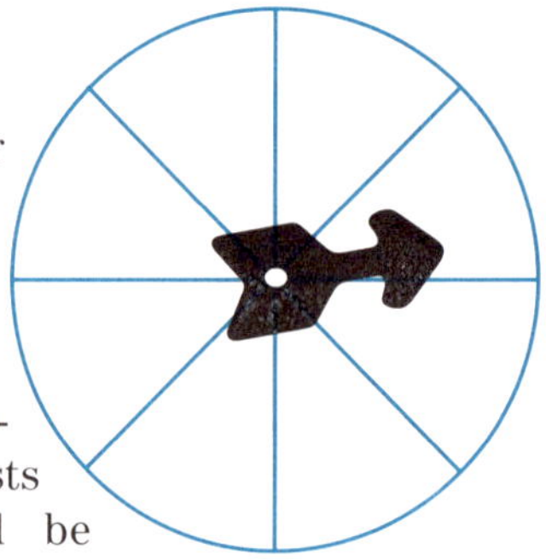

Divide a pizza circle or circle of posterboard into six to eight pie segments. Cover with clear contact paper. Add a spinner. After the spinner is laminated, prayer requests and/or instructions will be added to the segments with a marker. This will be used in most of the *POWer hours* this unit to help the children pray specifically.

Always meet early to go over plans with your staff and pray.

Kissed By an Angel

Fran Todd

POWer hour 10 dealing with rejection is probably the best time to read or tell this story to the children. But, it may be used anytime during this unit.

Debra was having a difficult day. There seemed to be lots of them lately. It was hard to smile—to think of a reason to smile. She could not remember when something inside her chest had not hurt. No, she was not sick—just heartsick. How long had Daddy been gone? The yelling and fussing between Mommie and Daddy had hurt, but this was worse.

School used to be fun, but now it seemed like all her friends could talk about was their moms and dads. This week some of the children's dads were coming to school to talk about their jobs. Then they were going to eat lunch with their children. What a stupid idea!

When Miss Beaver called her into the office, Debra was sure she was in trouble. But Miss Beaver only asked Debra if she could help her. She wanted to know if Debra wanted to talk about what was bothering her. No, Debra did not want to talk. It would not help, and it hurt too much.

Then Miss Beaver said something that sounded a lot like what her Mommie used to say—before Mommie lost her smile, too. Miss Beaver said, "Debra, maybe your guardian angel can fix your 'smiler.'" Her Sunday school teacher talked about angels, too. If only her angel could fix the big hurt in her chest and help her swallow the lump in her throat. Miss Beaver hugged Debra and sent her out to play.

Debra went outside, but she did not feel like playing. She sat on a bench near the fence. The sun peeked out from behind a fluffy cloud until it was shining brightly. The warmth felt good. She watched the shadows dance across the playground.

She tried to pray. Mommie said, "Just talk to God. He listens." She was wondering if God told her guardian angel what to do.

Debra jumped as someone tapped her shoulder. Oh, it was the little lady from the prayer chapel across the street. She held a big purple iris in her hand. Debra had often seen her tending the flowers around the chapel, but she had never seen her up close. The lady was older than Debra had thought, but oh, so beautiful. Her mother said there was something beautiful about everyone. Debra could not take her eyes off the old woman's hair. It was white and glistening, like a halo.

Debra realized the lady was speaking to her. "I am sorry if I frightened you, dear. I wanted to tell you that God said things will get better. Life will not always be as difficult as it is now." Gently, she kissed Debra's forehead. She handed Debra the flower, then turned and walked away.

Debra jumped up and ran to show the flower to Miss Beaver.

"It's lovely," Miss Beaver said. "Where did you get it?"

Debra turned to point to the lady, but she was gone! She had not had time to get back to the prayer chapel. She had disappeared.

The little girl looked up at her teacher and smiled. She knew she had been kissed by an angel . . . and her smiler was fixed!

Unit Three Go for the Gold

10

Memory Passage: I John 5:4

Unit Aim: To show how people in the Bible overcame in situations similar to ones faced by children today.

HURDLING REJECTION

Joseph Keeps a Right Attitude

Scripture Text: Genesis 37:3-4, 23-28, 45:1-5, 15; John 6:37

A right attitude can make rejection bearable and eventually turn it into acceptance.

Schedule

Date: _____

I. POWer of Worship (25-30 minutes)
   A. Clipboard (8 minutes)
      • A Word from the Lord
      • Scene I: Guardian Angels
      • Announcements
   B. Warm-ups (5 minutes)
      • Choruses about Heaven
   C. Exercise: AIM (4 minutes)
      • Story of Oma Ellis
      • Offering
   D. Knee Bends (4 minutes)
      • Prayer Spinner
   E. Scene II: Guardian Angels (4 minutes)
   F. Pushups (3 minutes)
   G. Truth Conductor (5 minutes)
      • Joseph's Coat of Many Colors
II. POWer of the Word (25-30 minutes)
   A. Training in the Word (4 minutes)
   B. Truth Conductor (4 minutes)
      • Puppet Play: The Golden Rule
   C. Spirit Generator (2 minutes)
   D. Illustrated Sermon (7 minutes)
      • Joseph Keeps a Right Attitude
   E. Invitation and Prayer (5-? minutes)
   F. Review
      • Biblical Calisthenics
      • Story: "Kissed by an Angel"

On Your Mark

✓ Are the gates of "heaven" up and open?
✓ From yellow construction paper cut a star-shaped name tag for each child. Or purchase star note pads from a Christian bookstore or school supply house. (Note: School supply houses are wonderful resource centers for church teachers. Even if you have to drive several miles to reach one, it is worth the trip.)
✓ Make copies of the scripts for the angels, Joseph, and the puppeteers. Joseph can be played by the teacher, a trainer, or drop-in guest. He wears a biblical robe. Have a practice session of angels' parts and the puppet play.
✓ Out of colored paper, cut six pieces in the shape of Joseph's robe, as illustrated on page 71. For a flannelgraph lesson, glue bits of flannel to the back.
✓ Make the prayer spinner as instructed on page 66. Write on the segments: Praise God. Give thanks. Pray for missionaries. Pray for disabled. Pray for compassion. Love God. Pray for each other. Pray for your pastor.
✓ Cut a cloud, star, or angel from posterboard. Print

the memory verse on it. Add pictures where possible, *e.g.,* trophy for "victory," praying child for "faith." Do not use a globe for "world" since that is not the meaning. After the children memorize the verse, add it to the stage scenery to keep it in view. Make a flashcard which reads, "faith" on one side and "overcomer" on the other. Wrap a magazine in brown paper.
- ✓ Reproduce the art of a mansion from page 125 for the Glory Avenue display. (See the Unit page.) Write on each the name of a child who has been born again.
- ✓ Make the offering box and display as instructed on the unit page.
- ✓ The AIMer should read the mission story and be prepared to tell it.

POWer of Worship

Director's Clipboard (8 minutes)

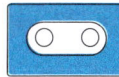

As the children enter, give each a star name-tag and tell them, "You are a star." Emphasize that they are winners and each is important to God.

Begin by asking the children to be very quiet as you have "A Word from the Lord" for them. Play the *kids POWer hour* tape. Show them how to find this passage, John 14:2-3, in their Bibles.

Introduce the unit "Heaven's Heroes" with Scene I from the skit, "Guardian Angels" on page 70.

Welcome guests. Introduce the activities planned for this unit and acknowledge birthdays. If there is time, have a free-for-all review quiz.

Warm-ups (5 minutes)

Teach the unit's theme song, "Angels Watchin' Over Me," from the *kids POWer hour* tape. Then allow the children to choose the songs about heaven or overcoming.

Exercise: AIM (4 minutes)

Not all missionaries are in foreign lands. Some are "home" missionaries. No matter where their field, missionaries are not always understood. Sometimes their greatest rejection comes from family and friends, rather than people in other lands.

When Oma Ellis was baptized in Jesus' name and received the Holy Ghost, her husband took their four children, ages seven months to eight years, and left her. For years Sister Ellis suffered rejection by her husband and his family, as she fought for her children. But she held onto her faith in God—it was that faith that made her an overcomer.

In 1929 when she had custody of her children, she pastored in Clarendon, Texas. During a severe snow storm, her family was out of food and nearly out of fuel. A rancher, a stranger, knocked on their door. "I felt compelled to ask how you were getting along. I've never done this before . . . I hope I won't offend you by offering some groceries to you," the kind stranger said.

"No, sir, we won't be offended," Sister Ellis assured him.

Soon the table was covered with boxes and sacks of groceries—everything they needed.

The man left, but almost immediately returned. "I have a feeling you need something else," he said.

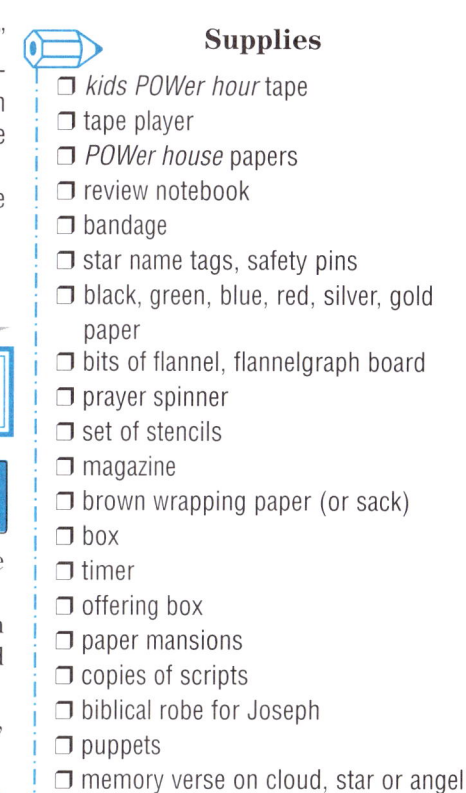

Supplies

- ☐ *kids POWer hour* tape
- ☐ tape player
- ☐ *POWer house* papers
- ☐ review notebook
- ☐ bandage
- ☐ star name tags, safety pins
- ☐ black, green, blue, red, silver, gold paper
- ☐ bits of flannel, flannelgraph board
- ☐ prayer spinner
- ☐ set of stencils
- ☐ magazine
- ☐ brown wrapping paper (or sack)
- ☐ box
- ☐ timer
- ☐ offering box
- ☐ paper mansions
- ☐ copies of scripts
- ☐ biblical robe for Joseph
- ☐ puppets
- ☐ memory verse on cloud, star or angel
- ☐ masking tape or Plasti-Tak®

PLUG-IN: When complimenting children during *kids POWer hour,* mention factors they can control, *e.g.,* their smile or posture, not "a fancy dress," or "new shoes." Certainly it is okay to comment on these things, but not when other children with less would feel intimidated.

This missionary story is condensed from *Pioneer Pentecostal Women* compiled by Mary H. Wallace, published by Word Aflame Press.

Guardian Angels

Scene I

Enter Angels, Alpha and Beta. Beta carries a pair of binoculars.

ALPHA: *Looks puzzled.* **What are you watching, Beta?**

BETA: *Motions toward audience.* **All these children, Alpha.**

ALPHA: **It's my job to watch over these children. God assigned that job to me.**

BETA: **I know!** *Still looking through the binoculars.* **Look! See those pretty girls and handsome boys.** *Might add specifics about "Gina's" lovely smile, "Greg's" good posture.*

ALPHA: **Beta, I don't need binoculars to see that!**

BETA: *Still looking through binoculars.* **Do you suppose they love God?**

ALPHA: **Just take a good look at their faces.**

BETA: *Scans audience with binoculars.* **Hummm. They do look clean, but what has that got to do with loving God?**

ALPHA: **When we love the Lord, it shows on our faces.**

BETA: **Really?** *Walks among the children, almost putting the binoculars in their faces.* **Yes, I can see that they are happy Christians.** *Walks back to the platform.*

ALPHA: **I thought you were Joseph's guardian angel.**

BETA: *Puts down the binoculars and says excitedly.* **Oh, I am.**

ALPHA: **You couldn't be watching over him if you have your eyes on everyone else.**

BETA: **You're right. Every time I take my eyes off him, he gets in trouble.**

ALPHA: **Then you had better focus on him.**

BETA: *Looks through binoculars.* **Oh, no! His brothers are pushing him around again! I better get down to earth and give him a hand.**

Exit Beta, on the run.

ALPHA: *Shakes head.* **Beta is always getting sidetracked.** *To audience.* **Oh, forgive me. I forgot to introduce myself. I know you so well—I have forgotten that you do not know me. I am your guardian angel for the next few** *kids POWer hours.* **My name is Alpha. My friend, who just left, is Beta. I'm here to help you learn to be a winner. You will be meeting people from the Bible who are winners and find out that they were very much like you. Go right ahead with** *kids POWer hour* **while I stand guard.**

Alpha stands guard in the back of the room or along one wall.

Scene II

ENTER Beta still carrying binoculars, with bandage over one eye and halo lop-sided. Alpha moves out to meet him.

BETA: **Oh, my eye!**

ALPHA: **What happened to you?**

BETA: **Boy, is Joseph ever in trouble.**

ALPHA: **What did he do?**

BETA: **It's not what he did. It's what they did!**

ALPHA: **They who?**

BETA: **His brothers. They pushed him around and called him names.** *Puts hand over eye.* **I tried to stop them—really I did. Oh, my eye!**

ALPHA: **I'm sorry about your eye.**

BETA: **God does not like it when people call one another bad names and get into fights. I hope He doesn't blame me for this.**

ALPHA: **You know God wouldn't blame you for something you couldn't help.**

BETA: **Well, I know it makes Him very sad when people fight and fuss.**

ALPHA: **I know. He wants people to get along with each other.**

BETA: **I was proud of Joseph. He didn't fight back or call his brothers bad names.**

ALPHA: **Then how did you get hurt?**

BETA: **I got in the way, trying to protect him.**

ALPHA: **That's a hazard of our jobs. It's part of a guardian angel's job description. I do hope Joseph is okay.**

BETA: *Looks through binoculars.* **Oh, no!**

ALPHA: **Now what?**

BETA: **He's in trouble again. I have to go.** *Exits.*

ALPHA: **I sure am glad you children are well-behaved. Might save me a black eye.** *Goes back to post, standing guard.*

PERMISSION TO COPY SCRIPT

"We could use some fuel," Sister Ellis told him. The man handed her enough money to buy fuel for the rest of the winter.

Oma Ellis suffered much from the rejection of her husband, but God provided her needs. She kept a right attitude and God used her miraculously. Many people were saved and healed under her ministry, and many churches were pioneered.

Later, after the children were grown, Sister Ellis' husband came to the Lord, and they were remarried. They spent fourteen happy years together before he died. Her life is proof that *a right attitude makes rejection bearable and eventually can turn it into acceptance.*

Oma Ellis was a winner—a soul winner. She hurdled rejection, overcame bitterness, and won a crown of life.

Musician plays. Ask the Angel Alpha to stand beside the offering box as the children march by and give.

Knee Bends (4 minutes)

Show the prayer spinner.

Ask for several volunteers to use the spinner and lead in prayer. A child spins and then prays aloud as directed on the spinner. "Lord Jesus, help our friends who are blind or crippled or disabled." "Thank you, Jesus, for my eyes." Do not expect flowery prayers. A sentence is sufficient. After the volunteers have prayed, lead the children in a closing prayer.

Guardian Angels: Scene II (4 minutes)

As soon as the children are seated, the Angel Beta bursts into the room for Scene II from page 70.

Pushups (3 minutes)

In a box or hat, toss a set of stencils, such as used for lettering on a bulletin board. Draw one. The children whose name starts with that letter jump to their feet and testify. Limit the testimony to one sentence. Set a timer for three minutes. Continue until time is called.

POWer of the Word

Training in the Word (4 minutes)

Show the cloud, star, or angel on which I John 5:4 is written. Read aloud together. *"For whatsoever is born of God overcometh the world: and this is the victory that overcometh the world, even our faith"* (I John 5:4).

To explain this verse, ask a child who has been "born again" to come to the front.

Darren has been born of God. He has repented, been baptized in Jesus' name, and received the Holy Ghost. Give child the sign "faith." Have him hold it so everyone can read it. **He has "faith" in God and obeys God's Word.**

But Darren still has battles to fight against sin—called in this verse "the world." Call another child to the front and give him a brown-paper wrapped magazine. **One day a friend offered Darren a dirty magazine.** Friend offers the magazine to Darren.

Joseph's Coat of Many Colors (5 minutes)

Option: This truth conductor can be used at the end of the session to lead into the altar call.

Give each piece of Joseph's coat to a child. As a color is needed, let that child bring it to the front and add it to the coat. If there is time, assign each verse to a reader.

Black—the earth was without form and void. Darkness was upon the earth (Genesis 1:2). Sin darkens the heart.

Green—green must be one of God's favorite colors. He put it everywhere. It represents new life (II Corinthians 5:17).

Blue—the color of truth. God's Word is true (Psalm 119:160). We can believe every word in the Bible.

Red—this is the color of blood. Jesus died on Calvary and shed His blood to pay for our sins (I Peter 1:19).

Silver—this represents the Holy Ghost, the Spirit of Christ, which dwells in us. Ask the children to quote together Acts 2:38.

Gold—a winner! Heaven is promised to all who overcome. We overcome through Jesus Christ (I John 5:4-5).

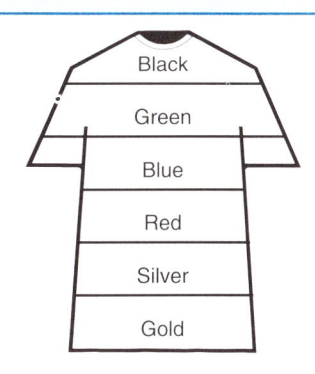

Darren knew this magazine contained pictures and stories which Christians should not read—dirty things that would pollute his mind. Because of *Darren's* faith—his love for Jesus—he told his friend, "No!" Child shakes head.

So *Darren* is an overcomer. Turn faith sign over to read "Overcomer." Have him wave the sign over his head victoriously as the class gives him a round of applause.

Read the verse together again two or three times. Add it to heaven's decor.

Puppet Play (4 minutes)

Use the puppet play, "The Golden Rule" on page 73 to introduce the Illustrated Sermon.

> **Spirit Generators**
> Lead the children in a worship chorus before the Illustrated Sermon. This quiets their spirits and prepares their hearts for the Word of the Lord.

ILLUSTRATED SERMON

Joseph Keeps a Right Attitude (7 minutes)

Use the script on page 74 to present the story of Joseph.

Invitation and Prayer (5-? minutes)

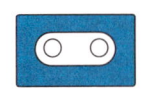

Replay "A Word from the Lord: John 14:2-3" from the *kids POWer hour* tape. **What do you think your mansion will look like?** Encourage responses.

As the musician plays, give children who have obeyed the plan of salvation a mansion to add to Glory Avenue. Have a helper stand beside Glory Avenue and give each child a ball of masking tape or Plasti-Tak® to place his mansion on the street.

Jesus wants every one to have a mansion in heaven. But we must be "born of God," that is, obey the plan of salvation first.

Invite children who have not repented or received the Holy Ghost to come forward to pray.

> **PLUG-IN**
> This activity may make those who have not obeyed the plan of salvation feel left out. We seldom want a child to feel that way. However, if feeling on the outside now will cause them to get in the church and be ready for the Rapture, then it certainly is worth the momentary uncomfortable feeling. That's why God sends conviction—a moment of pain for an eternity of life.

Review: Biblical Calisthenics

Use the remaining time to teach the children the Books of the Bible. Start by teaching the first five books of the Law.

Repetition is the key. Start by having them repeat after you, "Genesis, Exodus, Leviticus, Numbers, Dueteronomy." Ask for volunteers to stand and say them. Then call for the girls to say the first book, the boys the second, fifth graders the third, blondes the fourth, and everyone the fifth. Use variety. Keep them on their mental toes.

After a few minutes, have a review quiz, boys versus girls. Use questions, like these:

What is the second book of the Bible?
What book sounds like a song sang by two people, "a duet"?
What book makes you think of counting?

The Golden Rule

Puppets: Dynamo Girl and Man
Enter girl.

GIRL: Upset. **Just wait until I get my hands on her! I'll take her toys and break every one of them. When I see her bike, I'm going to kick it.**

Enter man.

MAN: **Who are you talking to—your guardian angel? I hope not.**
GIRL: **She's not an angel! She's a brat!**
MAN: **That wasn't a nice thing to say.**
GIRL: **That wasn't a nice thing for her to do.**
MAN: **Who are you talking about?**
GIRL: **I'm talking about Kayla. She got mad at me and threw my doll in her swimming pool. Her big brother had to save my doll.** Sobs. **Now my doll is all wet and soggy.**
MAN: **She will dry and be all right. What did you do to Kayla to make her so upset with you?**
GIRL: Puts head down. **I . . . I . . . I didn't do anything.**
MAN: **Are you sure about that?**

Girl keeps head down.

MAN: **You know Jesus sees all you do. He hears everything you say.**
GIRL: Looks up. **I only did one little thing.**
MAN: **And what was that?**
GIRL: **When Kayla wasn't looking, I sprayed her with the water hose.** Giggles. **It got her hair wet, and she really looked funny.**
MAN: **That's wasn't nice, was it?**
GIRL: **I guess not. But she shouldn't have thrown my doll in her swimming pool. She knows that's my favorite doll.**
MAN: **Do you remember the golden rule?**
GIRL: **The golden ruler? I don't have a golden ruler.**
MAN: **I did not say "ruler." I said, "rule." It is a special law which Jesus gave us. It says that we are to treat others like we want to be treated.**
GIRL: **What does that mean?**
MAN: **It means exactly what it says. We are to treat others like we want to be treated. You wouldn't want Kayla to spray you with the water hose, would you?**
GIRL: **She better not! I'll throw . . . Oh, I see what you mean.**
MAN: **Do you think you should find Kayla and ask her to forgive you?**
GIRL: **Forgive me? She ought to ask me to for . . . Oh, that golden ruler says . . . .**
MAN: **Golden rule.**
GIRL: **Yeah, that golden rule says that if I want her to ask me to forgive her, then I should ask her to forgive me. Right?**
MAN: **Right!**
GIRL: Takes deep breath. **That will be hard.**
MAN: **Why don't you ask God to help you?**

Puppets bow their heads.

GIRL: **Lord Jesus, I know it was wrong for me to spray Kayla with the water hose. Help me do right and ask her to forgive me. And because I want her to forgive me, I forgive her—even before she asks. In Jesus' name. Oh, one more thing, will You forgive me, too? Thanks. Amen.**

Exit both.

PERMISSION TO COPY

Joseph Keeps a Right Attitude

Joseph walks up to the sign pointing toward gate of heaven. He stops and speaks.

Hello, my name is Joseph. I am the eleventh son born to my father, Isaac. Imagine having ten brothers! It's a miracle I made it to heaven. My mother was a beautiful lady named Rachel. My parents were both old when I came along, so I was made to feel special. *Cups hands around mouth and whispers to audience.* **Some thought I was a bit spoiled.**

When I turned seventeen, my father gave me an expensive coat of many colors. This made my ten older brothers extremely jealous. At times, I felt they wanted to kill me. When my dad was not looking, they made fun of me and pushed me around. I wanted to treat them like they were treating me, but I knew that would not be pleasing to God.

One day my father sent me to check on my brothers who were watching the sheep. As I walked, I marveled at the wonderful world God had made for us. I thought about how much God loves us to give us such a beautiful place to live. I knew that even if my brothers rejected me, God had not. I decided that I was going to keep a right attitude and please God, no matter what it cost me.

As I approached my brothers, I heard them talking about me. I kept a smile on my face. "Here comes daddy's little pet," they called. Others mocked, "He's nothing but a dreamer." "My, my, look at the little king in his royal coat."

They pushed me to the ground. I saw the hate in their eyes. Before I knew it, they threw me in a dry well. I wanted to scream for help, but I knew they would only laugh and call me "a cry baby."

Later when they pulled me out of the well, I thought they were sorry for what they had done. But, no! Instead they sold me to a band of Ishmaelites going to Egypt.

Imagine being torn away from your home and sent with strangers—not knowing where you were going. Imagine being kidnapped and not knowing if you would ever see your parents again. That's what happened to me because my brothers hated me. Rejection is a terrible thing. It is like a sharp knife that pierces through your heart. It hurts.

I cried myself to sleep night after night. I was so glad my father had taught me about the one true God. The Lord God was the only Friend I had left. I talked to Him often.

In Egypt I was sold as a slave. I worked hard and soon received a promotion. Then I was thrown into prison for something I did not do. It seemed every way I went, I was rejected and falsely accused. But I stuck to my decision to keep a right attitude. Oh, sure, I had to pray a lot—a whole lot—to keep from becoming bitter and angry at the people who hurt me. I knew keeping a right attitude could make rejection bearable.

After several years in prison, God miraculously promoted me to the second ruler in the land. Overnight I went from the prison to the palace. This would never have happened if I had become bitter and fought for my rights. Because I let God fight my battles, I enjoyed a great victory.

One day my brothers came to Egypt for food. Immediately, I recognized them, but they did not know me. After all, it had been almost twenty years since they had sold me as a slave. They certainly did not expect to see me in the palace in a king's robe.

When I realized they were changed men, I told them who I was. They were scared half to death! They thought I would treat them like they had treated me.

But, no! I had no intention of harming them. They were my brothers and I loved them. I made a place for them and their families in Egypt where they had plenty of food. And after all those years, I saw my father again! A right attitude made rejection bearable and eventually turned it into acceptance.

As Joseph finishes, the angels step to each side of the gate of heaven.

BETA: *Blows trumpet.* **Hear ye! Hear ye! Joseph, step forward to receive your reward.**
Joseph slowly walks toward the gate. Musician plays soft background music.

ALPHA: *Opens scroll or Book of Life.* **Joseph, servant of the living God, because you kept a right attitude toward your brothers who hated you and because you lived for the Lord under extremely difficult circumstances, you are declared a winner. Because of your faith, you have won the victory over the world. Let's all stand.**
As children stand, the angel crowns Joseph and/or gives him a trophy.

ALPHA: **Great is your reward, for heaven is promised to "him that overcometh."**
Angels open the gate to heaven and Joseph enters. Gate closes behind him.

BETA: **Let's raise our hands and praise the Lord for the promise we have of heaven.**

PERMISSION TO COPY SCRIPT

> If there is time, read the story, "Kissed by an Angel" from page 67.

Finally, have a sword drill, using only these five books. Do not ask the children to read all the verse. Simply have them stand when they find it, repeat the reference, and read the first three words. Example: "Find Exodus 20:4." When a child finds it, he stands and calls out, "Exodus 20:4. Thou shalt not."

Trainers should move among the children, helping the preschoolers and slow readers.

Give each child a *POWer house* paper as he leaves.

Alternate Plans

(A) The closing emphasis could be placed on attitude rather than salvation, depending upon the needs of the children. Some may be suffering rejection at school—or home. These children desperately need to know that Jesus will never reject them.

A demonstration could be given showing ways to "hurdle" rejection, *e.g.*, prayer, returning good for evil, a right attitude.

If an AA—attitude adjustment—is needed by some, this would be a good time to pray with them. And it is a good time to give yourself an attitude check-up.

(B) Use Joseph's Coat of Many Colors on page 71 to lead into the invitation.

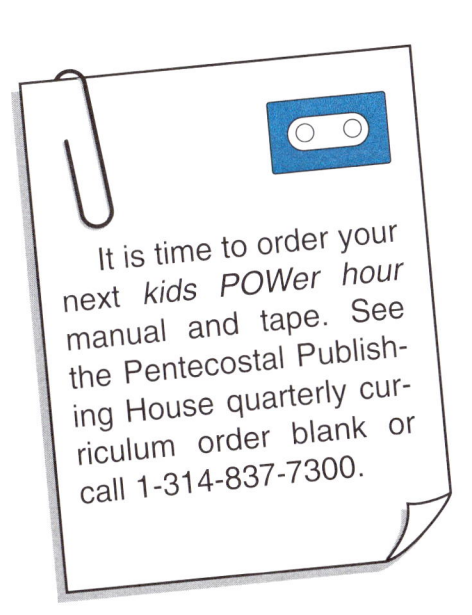

It is time to order your next *kids POWer hour* manual and tape. See the Pentecostal Publishing House quarterly curriculum order blank or call 1-314-837-7300.

Unit Three — Go for the Gold

11

Memory Passage: I John 5:4

Unit Aim: To show how people in the Bible overcame in situations similar to ones faced by children today.

CONQUERING PEER PRESSURE

Daniel and the Hebrew Children Take a Stand

Scripture Text: Daniel 1:8-21

A stand for right brings great rewards.

Schedule

Date: _____

I. POWer of Worship (25-30 minutes)
  A. Clipboard (8 minutes)
   • A Word from the Lord
   • Biblical Calisthenics
   • Announcements
   • Skit: A Hungry Angel
  B. Warm-ups (6 minutes)
   • Puppet Sing-along
  C. Knee Bends (3 minutes)
   • Prayer Spinner
  D. Exercise: AIM (5 minutes)
   • Story of Mable Hensley
   • Offering
  E. Pushups (4 minutes)
  F. Truth Conductor (3 minutes)
   • The World's Mold
II. POWer of the Word (25-30 minutes)
  A. Training in the Word (5 minutes)
  B. Spirit Generator (2 minutes)
  C. Illustrated Sermon (8 minutes)
   • Daniel and His Friends Take a Stand
  D. Taking a Stand (8 minutes)
  E. Invitation and Prayer (5-? minutes)
  F. Review
   • Right or Wrong?

On Your Mark

✓ On construction paper make signs of things the children should stand for or against, *e.g.,* honesty, obedience, kindness, respect, drugs, tobacco, liquor, dirty magazines, lying, cheating, movies. Attach each to a paint stirrer (available at most paint stores) or a ruler. Place in a box with handles sticking up so the children cannot read them. Make enough signs so each child has one.

✓ Make copies of the scripts for the angels and Daniel. Have a practice session.

✓ Divide I John 5:4 into phrases of three or four words. Print each phrase on a flashcard. Make two sets of different colors.

✓ Divide your expected attendance by three. Make an equal amount of question marks, exclamation marks, and periods from fluorescent paper. Make a large sign of each in matching color for the director. As the children enter, let each choose a sign and pin it to his shirt.

✓ Change the wording on the prayer spinner to: Pray for a missionary kid. Pray for your pastor. Praise God. Pray for abused children. Give thanks for loving parents. Ask for power to stand for right. Pray for a friend. Pray for your teacher.

✓ A trainer should be prepared to read the missionary story. He should be well enough acquainted with the story that he can maintain eye contact with the children.
✓ If you do not have a crown in your supply closet, make one to pass around during the testimony time.
✓ Cover a small steel ball with a layer of clay or play dough for the object lesson.

Supplies

- ❏ *kids POWer hour* tape
- ❏ tape player
- ❏ *POWer house* papers
- ❏ review notebook
- ❏ copies of scripts
- ❏ fluorescent paper
- ❏ pins
- ❏ sandwich
- ❏ construction paper
- ❏ paint stirrers or rulers
- ❏ box
- ❏ prayer spinner
- ❏ timer
- ❏ offering box
- ❏ paper mansions
- ❏ balloon for every child
- ❏ crown
- ❏ clay or play dough
- ❏ small steel ball
- ❏ copies of scripts
- ❏ biblical robe for Daniel
- ❏ puppets

POWer of Worship

Director's Clipboard (8 minutes)

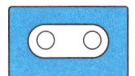

Announce that each child who behaves like a lady or gentleman will receive a reward (balloon) at the end of *kids POWer hour*.

Start the session with riddle time. Hold up the large question mark. Tell the children that as you play "A Word from the Lord," everyone wearing a question mark should listen for the mystery word that answers this riddle. Only children with a question mark are eligible to answer this riddle.

What is the mystery word?
When no one is fighting and all is still,
This word tells what we feel. peace

Next hold up the exclamation point and ask the children wearing one like it to solve this riddle as you replay the tape.

What is the mystery word?
It's what we feel when Jesus is near.
It's a happy word that rhymes with hear. cheer

For the final mystery word, hold up the period. Tell the children that this time you are going to give them a clue instead of a riddle. Place several large objects on the floor and step over them. Replay the tape. The mystery word is "overcome."

After the words are identified, show the children how to find John 16:33 and I John 5:4 in their Bibles. Point out that there are four Books of John in the New Testament.

Briefly review the first five books of the Bible.

Alpha and Beta, the guardian angels, enter and present the skit from page 78.

Warm-ups: Sing unto the Lord (6 minutes)

Use puppets to lead the singing and teach the children theme songs from the *kids POWer hour* tape.

For the Dynamo Special, have a puppet call up three or four children who usually do not participate to sing-along. Once they perform in a fun group like this a few times, they may be more willing to do a solo. This is not to punish them, but to encourage them to get involved, so do not make a big issue of it if they refuse.

Knee Bends (3 minutes)

Display the prayer spinner. Call for six children who are willing to lead in prayer. Each child should spin the pointer and pray a sentence prayer as instructed.

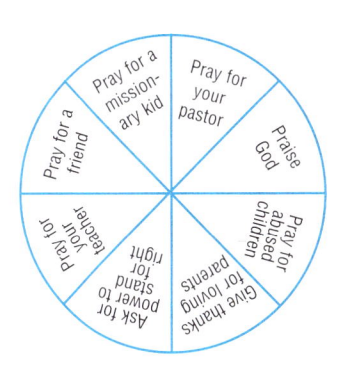

A Hungry Angel

BETA: Carries a sandwich and has binoculars hanging around his neck. **A guardian angel's work is never done. Now I am assigned to Daniel in Babylon. That's a long way from heaven, I'll tell you.** Takes bite of sandwich.

ALPHA: **What are you eating?**

BETA: Talks with mouth full. **It's bread and butter.**

ALPHA: **Don't you know it is not nice to talk with your mouth full?**

BETA: **Well, you asked me.** Gulps food down. **Sorry. I forgot.**

ALPHA: **Aren't you supposed to be standing guard over Daniel?**

BETA: **Yes, but he'll never miss me.** Looks through binoculars. **He's down there at King Nebuchadnezzar's palace at a banquet. You should see all the food they have spread out before him and his buddies.**

ALPHA: **What kind of food?**

BETA: Looks through his binoculars. **All kinds of meat and desserts and more desserts and more desserts. They are pouring wine into tall goblets. Knowing Daniel, he won't eat any of that food or drink that wine.**

ALPHA: **Are there any vegetables?**

BETA: **Vegetables? Alpha, are you kidding? Who needs veggies with all those desserts?**

ALPHA: **Everybody needs vegetables for a strong body. Nothing works right without vegetables.**

BETA: **Yuck! You can have this bread.** Gives it to Alpha. **I think I had better get down there and help eat the goodies.** Points to self. **Remember, I'm his guardian angel.** Exits.

ALPHA: Tries to stop him. **Wait! All that junk food will make you sick. Oh, well, I guess he will have to learn the hard way.**

Later in the session Beta should come in moaning and groaning with a stomach ache, and Alpha gets in another plug for a proper diet. **PERMISSION TO COPY SCRIPT**

Daniel and the Hebrew Children Take a Stand

Daniel, dressed in a biblical robe, walks up to the road sign and begins talking.

My name is Daniel. You probably have heard about when I was thrown in the den of lions, but something else happened to me which you may not have heard about.

My friends Hananiah, Azariah, Mishael, and I were taken prisoners of war to the foreign land of Babylon. We left our family and friends behind in our homeland of Judah. But we did not leave our God. He went with us.

Surprisingly, in Babylon my friends and I were treated well. Most prisoners-of-war are thrown in prison, but we lived in the palace and went to the university! The Babylonians wanted us to become one of them. They gave us Babylonian clothes to wear and taught us the Babylonian language. They even gave us Babylonian names. My new name was "Belteshazzar." I like Daniel better, don't you?

My three friends' new names were "Shadrach, Meshach, and Abednego." Have you heard of them before? I thought so. Remember the fiery furnace? Well, what I am telling you about happened before the fiery furnace incident.

The king wanted my three friends and me to eat the kind of food he ate. Fatty meats—which God had told us Jews not to eat. Rich desserts—which my parents had told me were not good for my body. And wine—yuck! Although the food looked delicious, I knew God did not want me to eat the king's food, for it was not good for me.

My family was far away, but who did I tell you went to Babylon with us? God. He was present, and I did not want to do anything to displease Him. So I told my three friends that we should not eat the king's food. They agreed. But how were we to get out of eating it without making the king mad? All the other young men in the king's court were eating the king's food. We prayed and God gave us a plan.

I asked the king's servant, "Please, sir, could we have water and vegetables to eat?"

He thought I was crazy, and all the other young men did, too. You should have heard them mock us. "Veggies? When you can have triple fudge cake and wine?" "What are you guys? Health food nuts?" "We've got some weird-o's here, for sure."

Finally, the servant agreed to let us try a vegetable diet for ten days. I knew that the king's food would only make us sluggish and slow, while a right diet would give us energy and sharpen our minds.

At the end of ten days we were healthier and felt better than anyone who had been eating the king's rich food. Everyone was surprised. The servant agreed to let us stay on our vegetable diet for the three years we attended the king's university.

When it was graduation time, guess who was at the top of the class? My friends and I. We were the smartest and healthiest young men in our class.

We took a stand for right and God greatly rewarded us—and the king did, too. We were given positions of honor in the Babylonian government.

Angels step forward.

BETA: Blows a trumpet. **Hear ye! Hear ye!**

ALPHA: **Step forward, Daniel, to receive your greatest reward.**

Daniel steps toward the gate of heaven. Music plays in the background.

ALPHA: Opens scroll. **Daniel, servant of the living God, because you took a stand for right, you have won the victory.**

BETA: Blows trumpet again. **Everyone stand.**

ALPHA: Places crown on Daniel's head and/or hands him a trophy. **Great is your reward, Daniel. Heaven is promised to the overcomer. Enter into eternal life.**

Daniel enters heaven and the gate closes behind him.

Lead the children in a song or prayer of praise as the gate closes behind Daniel. **PERMISSION TO COPY SCRIPT**

Or divide into prayer circles. Call for the youngest from each circle to spin the wheel to determine how his group prays.

Conclude by asking all the children to close their eyes, raise their hands, and praise the Lord.

Exercise: AIM (5 minutes)

"Put your hands up and come forward one at a time," came a stern command from a gruff voice out of the darkness! As she cautiously approached with hands up, the barrel of a rifle, with bayonet attached, suddenly loomed menacingly just inches from her face. "Who are you and where are you going?" spoke that same gruff voice, slightly more harshly now.

"We live at the mission house and we're going home," she answered softly. "I've been helping take care of a sick woman, one of your own Chinese women. She was giving birth to a baby and sent for me."

"You're not going by here. Just take one more step and I'll kill you!" bellowed the harsh voice as the man cocked his gun. She heard the click and knew the soldier meant business. He ordered another soldier to put a bayonet to her side.

Mable Hensley, a Pentecostal Assemblies of the World missionary in China, stopped dead in her tracks as she felt the pressure of the bayonet against her ribs. Confident that God would handle the situation and gaining courage, she breathed a quick prayer.

"You can't kill me unless my God lets you!"

"I'll show you I can kill you!" retorted the gruff-voiced man.

She spoke boldly, "You can't unless it is my time to go and God has a purpose for it. Otherwise, you can't kill me! Your gun can't kill me. Cock the trigger if you want to, but your gun cannot kill me."

The other soldiers yelled out, "Kill her! You've got her. Kill her!"

She turned to them. "He can't kill me! My God won't let him."

The gruff-voiced man peered at her momentarily, then turned to the soldier whose bayonet pressed against her side, and said, "Put your gun down. These foreign women aren't afraid of anything!"

Where did Mable Hensley get the courage to face such a challenge? Before this mission field experience, Mable had gazed down the barrel of another gun in an extremely frightening situation.

One night when she was ten years old, Mable was praying in the prayer room. A man came running in and said, "Sister Mable, come quick! My sister is at the altar seeking the Lord and her husband is here with a gun to kill her. Come quick and help us."

Standing between the man and his praying wife, Mable, with tears streaming down her cheeks, pleaded, "Please, don't do it. Please, don't do it. If you kill her, she'll go to heaven, but you will go to hell! Do you want to spend eternity in hell? Do you?"

As she spoke, the man pointed the gun at her. Still Mable pleaded with him. Suddenly, pressing the gun into her hands, the man fell to the floor, begging God for mercy. In a short time he received the Holy Ghost.

Later Mable asked the man who had come for her why he had called her instead of one of the men of the church. He replied that he felt the gunman would listen to a child more than a man.

Because Mable Hensley took a stand for right, God protected her. She learned a stand for right brings great rewards. Our Bible story is about some young men who learned the same lesson.

> This story is taken from "The Story of Carl and Mable Hensley," by Fred Kinzie in *Profiles of Pentecostal Missionaries,* compiled by Mary Wallace, published by Word Aflame Press. Used by permission.

As music plays, let the girls march around and give their mission offering. Count it and write it on a board for all to see. Then let the boys march around. Count and add their offering to the girls'. Ask the children to clap for joy because they were able to give to the kingdom of God.

Pushups: Testimony Time (5 minutes)

As music plays, the children pass a crown around the room. When the music stops, the child holding the crown puts it on, stands, and testifies. After a child testifies, he hands the crown to the one next to him and goes to stand along the wall. The music begins and the crown is again passed.

Continue until time is called or everyone has testified.

POWer of the Word

Training in the Word (5 minutes)

Show the children how to find I John 5:4 in their Bibles. Trainers should be seated among the children to help. Read aloud together two or three times.

Ask for as many volunteers as you have cards. Toss all the cards into the air. Players quickly pick up a card and divide into two teams, according to the color of their cards. First team to correctly put the verse together wins.

What is faith? Encourage children to give their definition.

What gives us power to overcome the world—or sin? our faith.

Faith in God gives us power to do what is right because we believe God's Word.

What did I promise you at the beginning of *kids POWer hour*? I said I would give a reward to everyone who behaves like a lady or gentleman today. Because you have faith that I will do what I said and you want a reward, you overcome the desire to poke your neighbor or stand on your head.

Because we believe what God says—His Word—we overcome the temptation to sin. We know that a stand for right brings great rewards.

Lead the children in a worship chorus to prepare them for the Word of the Lord.

> If Beta has not returned with a stomach ache, he should do so now because he needs to be in the room for the Illustrated Sermon. After a brief reminder from Alpha that he warned him, Beta should quickly recover so he can participate in the crowning of Daniel.
>
> The angels stand guard on either side of the gate to heaven.

The World's Mold (3 minutes)

Show two balls of clay or play dough. (One contains a steel ball.)

Ask an older child or trainer to read aloud Romans 12:2. Another translation of this verse says, "Don't let the world squeeze you into its mold."

Give each ball of clay the name of an imaginary child and develop a case study where they are being tempted. (Use a temptation which is relevant to your children.) One child has the Holy Ghost (the ball with the steel inside it); the other does not.

Apply pressure, trying to mold the clay into "the world's mold." Show how the Holy Ghost strengthened the one child so he did not conform to the world.

ILLUSTRATED SERMON

Daniel and the Hebrew Children Take a Stand (8 minutes)

Show the children how to find Daniel in their Bibles. Emphasize that the story they are about to hear is true.

Daniel uses the script from page 78 to tell his story.

Taking a Stand (8 minutes)

Daniel lived many years ago, but we still have to take a stand—for some things and against others.

Ask the children to march by the trainer holding the box of signs. Each child takes one sign. The child (or the trainer) reads the sign and asks: **Do we stand for or against this?** If it is something they should stand for, the child stands on your right. If it is something they should stand against, they stand on your left. Be sure they understand why each thing is right or wrong.

Organize a march. Those with a negative sign form a line and march around the room, chanting:

Down with sin. Down with sin.

The devil can't win. Down with sin.

After two or three rounds, the marchers replace their signs in the box and are seated.

Then the children with positive signs march chanting:

We stand for the right

With all our might.

Invitation and Prayer (5-? minutes)

After the marchers have returned to their seats, ask them to sit quietly with their heads bowed, eyes closed, and hands folded in their laps. Invitational music should be played in the background.

It is not always easy to stand for right and go against the crowd like Daniel and his friends did. Sometimes we fail and do things we know we should not do. This makes us feel guilty. It is a heavy, sad feeling inside us. No one likes to feel guilty.

The way to get rid of that guilt is to confess our sin to Jesus. We simply can tell Him, "Lord Jesus, I did wrong and I am sorry. Will You forgive me?" And He will. It is that simple.

Perhaps you are being tempted to do something you know is wrong. Your friends or classmates may be doing it and putting pressure on you to "go along with the crowd." Now is a good time to pray and ask the Lord to give you strength to do what is right.

Invite children who want to pray to come to the front. If no one responds, ask everyone to stand and lead the children in a congregational prayer before moving on to another activity.

Review

Use the questions from your review notebook to have a "Right or Wrong" quiz. Rephrase each question so that it is a statement. If the statement is right, the children stand up and spin around. If it is wrong, they sit frozen.

Give each child who has behaved like a lady or gentleman a balloon to use for his *POWer house* project as he leaves.

Remember to distribute the *POWer house* papers.

PLUG-IN: Any time a child is baptized in Jesus' name and receives the Holy Ghost, let him add his mansion to "Glory Avenue."

Unit Three   Go for the Gold

12

Memory Verse: I John 5:4

Unit Aim: To show how people in the Bible overcame in situations similar to ones faced by children today.

TACKLING FEAR

Esther Saves Her People

Scripture Text: Esther

Courage is fear that has said its prayers.

Schedule

Date: _____

I. POWer of Worship (25-30 minutes)
  A. Clipboard (6 minutes)
    • Discovering the Key Word
    • Puppet Skit
    • Announcements
  B. Warm-ups (6 minutes)
    • Sing unto the Lord
    • Dynamo Specials
  C. Knee Bends (3 minutes)
    • Overcoming Fear
  D. Skit: A Lovely Assignment (6 minutes)
    • A Special Surprise
  E. Pushups (5 minutes)
    • Showers of Blessings
  F. Exercise: AIM (3 minutes)
    • Offering
II. POWer of the Word (25-30 minutes)
  A. Training in the Word (5 minutes)
    • A Talk Show
  B. Spirit Generator (2 minutes)
  C. A Word from the Lord (3 minutes)
  D. Illustrated Sermon (8 minutes)
    • Esther Saves Her People
  E. Invitation and Prayer (5-? minutes)
  F. Review
    • Biblical Calisthenics

On Your Mark

✓ Make copies of the *POWer house* papers, the scripts for the angels, and Esther. Have a practice session. Esther is dressed in royal apparel. If you are giving a crown to those who enter heaven, make sure the crown Esther wears is smaller and not as pretty.

✓ For the Pushups make as many 3" raindrops from construction paper as you want children to testify. Put these in a bucket and lay a piece of waxed paper on top of them. Place a dipper containing a small amount of water in the bucket. Hide the bucket from the children.

✓ Write each letter "C-O-U-R-A-G-E" on an index card. Make two sets.

✓ Make enough construction paper hearts so there is one for each girl. Fold hearts. Put a star inside one heart. Place all in a basket. Purchase a small heart-shaped box of chocolates or a large candy bar.

✓ Change the words on the prayer spinner to things children fear, *e.g.,* the dark, storms, being left out, speaking before an audience, being laughed at.

✓ The Scripture text is the entire Book of Esther. While this is a lengthy reading, it is important to review the whole story before this session. Of course, everything will not be taught to the children. A good teacher always knows more than he teaches.

POWer of Worship

Supplies
- ☐ *kids POWer hour* tape
- ☐ *POWer house* papers
- ☐ review notebook
- ☐ red construction paper
- ☐ basket
- ☐ small heart-shaped box of chocolates
- ☐ copies of scripts
- ☐ index cards
- ☐ prayer spinner
- ☐ bucket
- ☐ waxed paper
- ☐ dipper
- ☐ raindrops
- ☐ table and chairs for panel
- ☐ microphone, real or toy
- ☐ puppet
- ☐ royal robe and crown for Esther

Director's Clipboard (6 minutes)

Call for older children, two boys and two girls. Explain that it is boys versus girls to see who can be the first to discover today's key word. Give each pair a set of scrambled index cards. They are to unscramble the word. The first pair to correctly spell "courage" wins. Give them a round of applause. Then give the other team a round of applause for participating.

As you talk, a puppet should peek over the edge of the puppet stage, look around, then quickly disappear. Ask the children to repeat several times with you the *POWer line*, "Courage is fear that has said its prayers."

Brave people are not people who are not afraid. Brave people are people who do courageous things even though they are afraid. When we are afraid, if we will pray, God will give us the courage we need to do whatever we have to do.

When it becomes "evident" that something is happening to distract the children, ask: **What is going on?** Children will tell you about the puppet. **A puppet? Where? I don't see . . .** Puppet appears and disappears quickly. **Oh, I see. Come on out here,** *(name).*

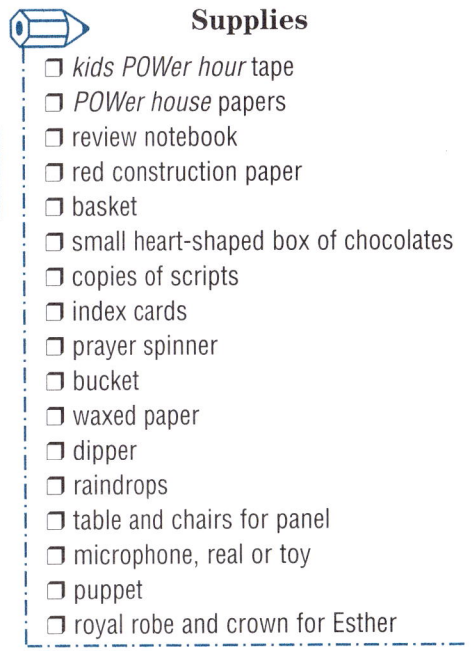

> Replace comments about fearing dogs with something that you fear because you will probably be asked about it later by the children.

PUPPET:	Wails in shaky voice from behind stage. **Oh, no. Please don't m-m-make me come out t-t-there.**
DIRECTOR:	**But why not? We want to see you.**
PUPPET:	**But I don't want to see you. I . . . I . . . I'm sssscared.**
DIRECTOR:	**Scared? What is there to be scared of?**
PUPPET:	**All those k-k-kids.**
DIRECTOR:	**These kids? You're scared of these kids? They won't hurt you. Will you, kids? They like you.**
PUPPET:	**I know. Actually, I'm not scared of the kids. I'm scared of . . . of. . . .**
DIRECTOR:	**Of what?**
PUPPET:	**Well, this may sound s-s-silly, but I'm s-s-scared of talking in front of those k-kids.**
DIRECTOR:	**Oh. Lots of people are afraid of speaking in front of an audience. Tell you what. You come out but turn your back to everyone. Then you won't see them.** PUPPET enters and turns back to audience.
DIRECTOR:	**How's that?**
PUPPET:	**Okay, I guess. But I sure miss seeing all the pretty girls.**
DIRECTOR:	**Then turn around.**
PUPPET:	Starts to turn around two or three times, then changes his mind. **Well, I'll try. . . . No, I'm just not brave enough to face them.** Wails. **I'm the world's biggest coward . . . a big baby . . . I'm just chicken! Cluck-cluck-cluck. See I even sound like one.** Sobs. **Oh, Jesus, help me!**
DIRECTOR:	**Everyone is afraid of something,** *(name).*
PUPPET:	**Really? What are you afraid of?**
DIRECTOR:	**Me? I'm afraid of *dogs*. When I was a child, I was bitten by one and had to have stitches in my leg. Ever since then I've been terrified of dogs, all sized dogs.**
PUPPET:	Turns around amazed. **You're scared of dogs? A big person like you is scared of a little bitty chihuahua?**
DIRECTOR:	**I really am.**
PUPPET:	Brags. **I'm not scared of *dogs*. Are you, kids?** Children respond. **What are you afraid of?** As the children respond, the puppet converses with three or four of them something like this. *You're afraid of the dark? Boy, I am, too. But you know what I do?*

> *Every night I pray that the Lord will protect me. Then I go to bed and go to sleep.*
>
> *You're afraid of storms? Me, too. When it storms, I remember how Jesus calmed the storm on the sea for the disciples, and I ask Him to calm the storm. And you know what? Sooner or later, the storm always stops.*
>
> DIRECTOR: *(Name)*, what you are doing?
>
> PUPPET: What am I doing?
>
> DIRECTOR: Yes, what are you doing?
>
> PUPPET: Why, I'm talking to these ki.... Puts hands over mouth and quickly turns his back to audience. **I'm talking to these kids.** Slowly turns back around to face the children. **And I'm not even scared! I'm not afraid!** Jumps up and down, singing. **I'm not afraid! I'm not afraid! I'm big and brave. I'm not afraid!**
>
> DIRECTOR: Isn't it surprising how when we forget about ourselves and think of others, we often lose our fear?
>
> PUPPET: It's more than that. I prayed. Remember I said, "Oh, Jesus, help me." It wasn't a big prayer, but it was a real one. Jesus heard and helped me. Kids, do you remember the *POWer line*? Say it with me. **Courage is fear that has said its prayers.** Remember that, kids. See you later.
>
> PUPPET exits.
>
> PERMISSION TO COPY SCRIPT

PLUG-IN: Are any of your children poets or story tellers? Do any of them have exceptional memories? Encourage them, as well as children who are musical, to use their talents during Dynamo Special time.

Make announcements, acknowledge birthdays, and welcome guests.

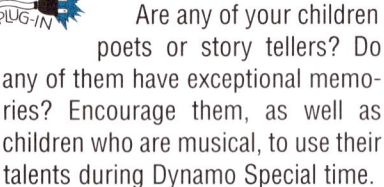

Warm-ups: Sing unto the Lord (6 minutes)

"Whisper a Prayer"
"Angels Watchin' Over Me"
"Greater Is He That Is in Me"

Have as many Dynamo specials as time allows. It may be necessary to limit the singers to two or three verses per song.

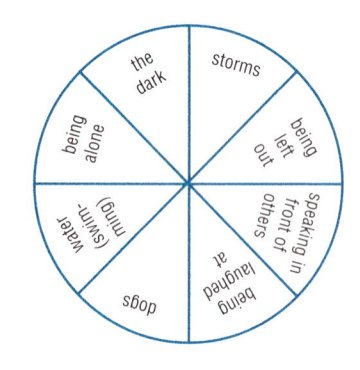

Knee Bends: Prayer Spinner (3 minutes)

Take prayer requests and lead in a congregational prayer.

Then as you turn the pointer on the prayer spinner, ask everyone who is afraid of the thing that is named to raise their hands. Help the children overcome their shyness by starting with an item that you fear, such as speaking before an audience.

Lead the children in prayer for each fear. Conclude with a "praise break," thanking God for helping us overcome our fears.

(Prayer spinner wheel: the dark, storms, being left out, speaking in front of others, being laughed at, dogs, water (swimming), being alone)

Skit: A Lovely Assignment (6 minutes)

Use the script on page 85 to present this skit.

Pushups: Showers of Blessings (5 minutes)

Bring out the bucket of raindrops, being sure the children do not see inside it. Pretend it is full of water. Briefly and simply compare water to the Holy Ghost—it satisfies our thirst. Drink all the water in the dipper, letting a little run down your chin so the children see.

Ask who wants a drink. As you start toward a child to give him or her a drink, pretend to stumble. Bring the bucket up and hold the dipper so it does not fly out and hit someone. Send the raindrops showering on the children. They will be expecting to be splattered with water.

After the excitement has settled, ask the children to pick up a raindrop (one per child) near them. Call for those with raindrops to testify about a

A Lovely Assignment

Enter both Angels. Beta has binoculars around his neck and is carrying a basket of construction paper hearts and a Bible. He is smiling and looks dreamy.

ALPHA: **What are you up to now, Beta?**

BETA: **Oh, Alpha, I have been given the loveliest assignment. I'm going to be a matchmaker.**

ALPHA: **A matchmaker? Why in the world are you going to make matches? There are already millions, even billions, yeah, trillions of matches on the earth already. I would think you had more important things to do—like standing guard.**

BETA: **You're all mixed up, Alpha. I am not going to make matches—like matches which hurt children when they play with them. I am going to make a love match.**

ALPHA: **A what?**

BETA: **A love match. You see, there is this beautiful girl I have been assigned to guard. She loves God and is obedient.**

ALPHA: **Sounds like an easy assignment to me. Who is she?**

BETA: **Her name is Esther. She is the prettiest girl in the land. My job is to protect her and see that she and the king fall in love.**

ALPHA: **Sounds like a fairy tale to me.**

BETA: **But it's not. It's a true story from the Bible. In fact, there is a book in the Bible with her name.** Shows Bible. **It is just before the Book of Psalms. Who remembers how to find the Book of Psalms?** Children should respond that you open your Bible to about the middle. **Did you bring your Bible to** kids POWer hour? **Great! Let's find Esther. First, find the Book of Psalms. Now turn back toward the front of the Bible just a little bit. Go slowly because Esther is not a very big book.** Shows children how to find Esther.

ALPHA: **Wow! You have been given an important assignment. Imagine being assigned to someone who has a book of the Bible named after her.**

BETA: **Oh, it's not the first time I've had someone like that. Who was I guarding last** POWer hour, **kids? Daniel. Let's see who can be the first four kids to find Daniel in their Bible. When you find it, stand up and hold your open Bible over your head.**

After four children have found Daniel and been congratulated, continue.

ALPHA: **Now back to your love story. Did I get this straight? You are supposed to make Esther and the king fall in love?**

BETA: Nods and hands basket to Alpha. **Would you hold this basket for me while I see where Esther is now?** Looks through binoculars.

ALPHA: **What's in this basket?**

BETA: **It's full of hearts of love. There is one special heart in it. The girl that gets it is going to get a special surprise.**

ALPHA: **I hope I get it.**

BETA: Continues to look through binoculars. **I told you it's for a girl, not you. You're an angel. Remember?**

ALPHA: **I remember, but sometimes I wish I was human. The nicest things happen to people. They get to receive the Holy Ghost, and angels don't.**

BETA: **I know. People are really special to God.**

ALPHA: **What's Esther doing?**

BETA: **There are lots of girls lined up outside the palace. Oh, there's Esther. She stands out from the rest like a star among . . . among rocks. I can see the beauty of the Lord shining through her from way up here.**

ALPHA: **Surely the king will choose her to be his queen.**

BETA: Puts binoculars down. **If he has any sense, he will.**

ALPHA: **How did you get this assignment?**

BETA: **Esther's adoptive father has been praying for God to protect her. So God sent me to answer Mordecai's prayers.**

ALPHA: **Do you think you can pull off this match making? Don't you think that's God's job?**

BETA: **Yes, but I don't mind helping out a bit.** Looks through binoculars again. **Oh, no!**

ALPHA: **Now what?**

BETA: **All those girls are pushing and shoving. Poor Esther, she's going to get hurt if I don't get down there right away and protect her.** Starts to exit.

ALPHA: **Wait! What about your basket?**

BETA: **That's for you to give the girls. There's a winning heart in that basket. The girl who gets it gets a special surprise. Bye. Here I come, Esther. Don't be afraid.**

ALPHA: **But, Beta, aren't you afraid to go down there in the middle of all those pushing, shoving girls?**

BETA: **Yes, but I've said my prayers. And remember the** POWer line. **Courage is fear that has said its prayers.**

Beta exits. Alpha lets each girl choose a heart from the basket. He tells them not to open their heart until everyone has one. The girl who receives the heart with the star on it is also given a small heart-shaped box of chocolates.

PERMISSION TO COPY SCRIPT

blessing the Lord has showered on them. Give an example of a blessing the Lord has given you to help them understand the concept.

Exercise: AIM (3 minutes)

Refer to past missionary stories. Ask discussion questions, emphasizing that missionaries have fears just like everyone else. Briefly fill in important details as you feel necessary, especially if many have not heard the story, or heard it recently.

How do you think ten-year-old Mable Hensley felt when the man threatened her with a gun?

How do you think she felt years later in China when the soldiers stuck a bayonet in her ribs?

What do you think Sister Oma Ellis feared when she took her four small children and started a church?

What do you think gave these missionary ladies the courage to do what they needed to do?

What is the *POWer line*? Courage is fear that has said its prayers.

Announce the total of the missionary offerings. Remind the children that next *kids POWer hour* will be their last opportunity to give to this project.

Let the children march and sing, "Give and Pray," as they give their offering.

> If there is time, review the missions cheer on the *kids POWer hour* tape, which the children learned in the first unit.

POWer of the Word

Training in the Word (5 minutes)

> Set up a table and three or four chairs for the talk show panel.

Who wants to be on KUPC's talk show? Choose three or four children who have been present the last two *kids POWer hours*. Sit them at a table in the front of the room. Ask contestants review/discussion questions based on I John 5:4. Use a microphone (real or toy).

Welcome, ladies and gentlemen, to radio's best talk show. I am your host, *(name)*. I would like for our panel to introduce themselves and tell us their age. Children on the panel do so.

Our discussion today centers around a wonderful, powerful verse of Scripture which we have been learning at *kids POWer hour*. If the panelists are ready, we will begin.

Who remembers the memory verse for this unit?

Where is it found?

What does it mean to be "born of God"?

What does it mean to "overcome the world"?

What gives us victory to overcome sin?

Who would volunteer to tell us about a time you were tempted to do wrong?

What stopped you from doing wrong?

Have you been "born of God"? Would you tell us about your experience when you received the Holy Ghost?

How does believing God's Word help us win victory over sin?

When the talk show is over, give the contestants a round of applause. Ask the children to find I John 5:4 in their Bibles. Give assistance as needed. Read together a couple of times.

A Word from the Lord (3 minutes)

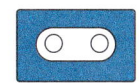

Now let's listen to "A Word from the Lord." Listen closely. Play II Kings 6:16 and Isaiah 41:13 from the *kids POWer hour* tape.

When the Lord said that there are more with us than with them, He was saying there are more for us than against us. Did you know that for every demon there are two angels? We do not have to be afraid of the devil and his demons. God and the angels are watching over us.

Take hold of a child's hand. **When the Lord said He would hold our right hand, He did not mean He would literally take hold of your hand, like I am holding *Amy's*. Right hand in the Bible means power and strength. Everyone hold up your right hand. Your right hand is strong if you are right-handed. You might use it to do most of your work. So when the Lord said that He would hold our right hand, He was saying that He would give us the strength to do whatever we have to do—speak in front of a class, go into a dark room, keep calm in a storm.**

Play the tape one more time.

> **Spirit Generators:** Lead the children in a worship chorus before the Illustrated Sermon to prepare their hearts for the Word of the Lord.

ILLUSTRATED SERMON

Esther Saves Her People (8 minutes)

Our Bible story today is about Esther, a beautiful, courageous queen who had a frightening job to do.

Use the script on page 88 as a guide to present the Illustrated Sermon.

- - -

Invitation and Prayer (5-? minutes)

Before I received the Holy Ghost, one of my greatest fears was being left behind when Jesus comes for His church. When I received the Holy Ghost, that fear left me, and I was filled with joy and excitement. If you are afraid of being left behind, you can get rid of that fear today by being filled with the Spirit of the Lord.

Perhaps someone is afraid to come to the altar because others are watching you. If there is someone standing beside you who needs to pray but he is afraid to come alone, ask, "Would you like for me to go to the altar with you?"

Perhaps there are others here who have the Holy Ghost but you are still bothered by fear. You may be afraid of the dark, of dying, of the future, of being alone. Whatever your fear, come to the front and we will ask the Lord to take it away.

Ask the children to gather around and pray with their friends who want prayer. This can be an open, caring time with the children praying one for another.

> If you have children in your group who do not know the plan of salvation, explain it before making an altar call.

Review

Use extra time to help the children memorize the books of the Bible. They should know the first five books of the Old Testament. To learn the next seven use this memory key.

Esther Saves Her People

Esther enters and stands by the sign pointing to heaven. The angels stand guard on each side of the gate.

Is anyone here adopted? I was. When my parents died, my cousin, Mordecai, adopted me. He was a wonderful father who taught me about the one true God. We were Jews and honored God with prayer and fasting.

As I grew up, many people remarked about how beautiful I was. But Mordecai always told me that real beauty is on the inside. Has your mother ever told you, "Pretty is as pretty does"?

One day King Ahasuerus was looking for a bride. He wanted the fairest in the land. Sounds like a fairy tale, doesn't it? But it's not. It's true. Many girls, including me, were taken to the palace so the king could choose his new bride.

I could hardly believe it when I was chosen to be the queen! Imagine a Jewish orphan becoming queen of Persia. Oh, yes, I'd better tell you. We were aliens in Persia. My family originally lived in Palestine, but my ancestors had been taken prisoners-of-war. As the years went by, we Jews blended into the culture. Many people forgot that we were strangers in Persia because we looked liked everybody else. So, you see, it was a double miracle for me to become the queen. Mordecai said God had put me there for a reason, and he warned me not to tell the king that I was a Jew.

One day Mordecai sent word that two of the king's servants were plotting to kill the king. I told the king and the king's life was saved.

Then a problem arose. The king's top officer, Haman, did not like Mordecai because Mordecai would not bow before him. Mordecai said he bowed only to the one true God. This put Haman in a rage. He decided to get rid of Mordecai and all the Jews. He persuaded the king to sign a law that all the Jews were to be killed!

I did not know about this law until Mordecai sent me word. He wanted me to go before the king to ask him to save the Jews. Now that doesn't sound like a big deal to you—for a wife to ask her husband for a special favor. But it was different in my day.

No one—not even the queen—went into the king's presence unless the king sent for them. And the king had not sent for me in thirty days. I wasn't even sure he wanted to see me. When someone went into the throne room, if the king was happy to see them, he would hold out his golden scepter. If he was angry because the person had presumed to come without being invited, he would not hold out his scepter and that person was killed! It was life or death to go into the throne room uninvited!

I was scared! When I told Mordecai that the king had not called for me for thirty days, Mordecai reminded me that I was in the palace for a reason. I told him to send word that all the Jews were to fast and pray for three days, then I would go before the king. Those were the longest days of my life. I was so scared!

At the end of three days, I put on my prettiest robe and went trembling to the throne room. When the king turned and saw me standing in the doorway, I almost fainted. What was he going to do?

The king stared at me for several seconds—then slowly he started to smile and he raised the scepter. I was saved! The king had granted me favor. I invited the king to a banquet in his honor. He came at the proper time, and when the time was right to do so, I told the king of Haman's plans.

When I told the king about Haman's wicked plan, the king became very angry. He was surprised to discover that I was a Jew. But it did not matter to him that I was an alien. He loved me. He had Haman killed and spared my people. And Mordecai was promoted to a position of honor because he had once saved the king's life. My story has a fairy tale ending, but it is not a fairy tale. Every word is true.

People called me "courageous and brave." Actually, I was scared half to death. But I prayed and God helped me do what I had to do. So, you see, I wasn't brave, at all. But, I was smart—smart enough to pray.

Music plays.

BETA: *Blows trumpet.* **Hear ye! Hear ye! Queen Esther, step forward.**
Angels step forward to meet Esther as she stands before the gate of heaven.

ALPHA: **Queen Esther, servant of the living God, because you were brave and obedient—because you feared God and not man—because you overcame fear to save your people, you may enter into eternal life.** *He gives Esther a crown/trophy.* **Heaven is promised to the overcomer, and you are an overcomer! Enter and live forever.**
Esther enters heaven and gates close behind her.

PERMISSION TO COPY SCRIPT

Joshua Judges Ruth—a sentence.

To memorize the next four—I and II Samuel, I and II Kings—think of twin boys named, "Samuel Kings."

As simple as that, the children have learned the first twelve books of the Bible. Have a sword drill calling out the names of books only. Team preschoolers with older children.

Give each child a *POWer house* paper as he leaves.

Your next *kids POWer hour* manual should have arrived by now. Start making plans for the next series.

Unit Three — **Go for the Gold**

13

Memory Passage: I John 5:4

Unit Aim: To show how people in the Bible overcame in situations similar to ones faced by children today.

DEFEATING INFERIORITY

Gideon Wins the Battle

Scripture Text: Judges 6, 7

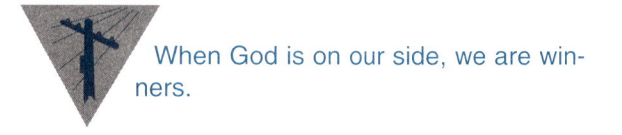

When God is on our side, we are winners.

Schedule

Date: _____

I. POWer of Worship (25-30 minutes)
   A. Clipboard (10 minutes)
      • Puppet Skit: Spiritual Warfare
      • Announcements
      • Review Game: Move Up
   B. Warm-ups (6 minutes)
      • Sing unto the Lord
      • Dynamo Specials
   C. Knee Bends (3 minutes)
      • Prayer Spinner
   D. Skit: An Angel at Attention (4 minutes)
   E. Pushups (3 minutes)
      • A Christian Soldier's Cheer
   F. Exercise: AIM (4 minutes)
      • Story of Laverne Collins
      • Offering
II. POWer of the Word (25-30 minutes)
   A. A Word from the Lord (4 minutes)
   B. Training in the Word (4 minutes)
   C. Spirit Generator (2 minutes)
   D. Illustrated Sermon (8 minutes)
      • Gideon Wins the Battle
   E. Invitation and Prayer (5-? minutes)
   F. Review
      • Move Up

On Your Mark

✓ Make copies of the *POWer house* papers and scripts.

✓ Have a practice session with the angels and Gideon.

✓ Puppeteers need to practice, "A Christian Soldier," with the *kids POWer hour* tape. Tape a copy of the script inside the puppet stage for puppeteers to follow.

✓ AIMer should be prepared to tell the missionary story.

✓ Change wording on prayer spinner to: a foreign missionary, a home missionary, evangelists, government leaders, school teachers, doctors, Sunday school teachers, pastors.

✓ Purchase pencils to give each child who can quote I John 5:4. They will need these to complete their *POWer house* project.

✓ Announce a planning session to finalize plans for the next *kids POWer hour* series.

POWer of Worship

Director's Clipboard (10 minutes)

Supplies
- ❏ *kids POWer hour* tape
- ❏ tape player
- ❏ review notebook
- ❏ *POWer house* papers
- ❏ puppets—girl and boy
- ❏ timer
- ❏ copies of scripts
- ❏ camouflage clothes, sword, shield, etc.
- ❏ pencils for awards
- ❏ biblical costume for Gideon

Start with this puppet skit, "Spiritual Warfare," from the *kids POWer hour* tape.

Spiritual Warfare

Enter Dynamo Girl.

GIRL: Looks around. **No, that's not him. That's not him either. Where is my friend. He usually isn't late. Has anyone seen my friend? I'd better go find him.** Exits.

Enter Dynamo Boy, dressed like a soldier.

BOY: Marching. **Hup 1-2-3, hup 1-2-3. At ease.** Looks all around. **She was supposed to meet me here. I wonder where she is? I'd better go find her.** Fades as he exits. **Hup 1-2-3, hup 1-2-3 . . . .**

Enter Dynamo Girl, looking around.

GIRL: **Still not here? It's not like him to be late. Where could he be? I'd better go call. He may have forgotten our plans.** Exits.

Enter Dynamo Boy.

BOY: **Hup 1-2-3, hup 1-2-3. At ease. I can't believe she's not here. Has anyone seen my friend?** Pause for children to respond. **You have? She was here? Maybe I'd better just sit down and wait for her. I'm tired.**

Enter Dynamo Girl.

GIRL: **There you are! I've been looking everywhere for you.**
BOY: **And I've been looking everywhere for you.**
GIRL: Puzzled. **Why are you dressed like that?**
BOY: Proudly. **I am a Christian soldier!** Marches. **Hup 1-2-3, hup 1-2-3, hup. . . .**
GIRL: **Really? I'm glad, but aren't you overdoing it a bit?**
BOY: **Look. We are fighting a spiritual battle. It's serious business. You can't overdo it! Hup 1-2-3, hup. . . .**
GIRL: **A spiritual war?**
BOY: **Yes. Way back before the beginning of time the devil was not the devil. He was Lucifer, a beautiful angel in Heaven.**
GIRL: **Really? The devil lived in heaven?**
BOY: **He sure did. Then he got jealous of God and power hungry. He wanted God's position.**
GIRL: **The devil wanted God's position? You mean, he wanted to be God?**
BOY: **Yep. So he staged a rebellion.**
GIRL: **A rebellion in heaven?**
BOY: **Yes. He persuaded one-third of the angels to join him in a war against God.**
GIRL: **Boy, that was stupid!**
BOY: **Sure was. And it didn't work. God and His angels whipped the socks off the devil and his angels.**
GIRL: Claps joyfully. **Bravo! I knew they would! Why, God could have defeated them single-handedly.**
BOY: **God kicked Lucifer and his army out of heaven down to this earth.**
GIRL: **Oh, no! I wish God had sent them to Mars. That's why there's so much trouble and evil on earth!**
BOY: **Right. Now we call him Satan, and he is a liar, a cheat, a murderer, a thief—everything that's bad.**
GIRL: **The Bible tells us to resist him and he will run from us.**

PERMISSION TO COPY SCRIPT

Review Quiz

Move Up

Arrange four chairs (or more) in front of the room one staggered behind the other, as shown.

```
            X
         X
      X
   X
```

Ask for volunteers to quiz. Start with the child in front. If he correctly answers the question, he moves to the back and each child moves up. If he misses, he is out. The other players move up and a new player is chosen from the audience and seated in the back chair. Continue until time is called or there are no more questions.

Use this game at the beginning of *kids POWer hour* for a review of past lessons, as well as the books of the Bible learned to date. Then play it again at the end of the session to review today's lesson.

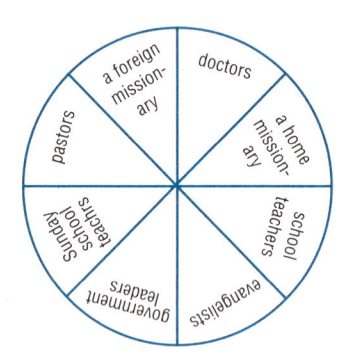

Children learn by example. Prayer in children's church should not always be congregational prayer. Occasionally, children need to bow their heads, close their eyes, and listen to an adult pray. This is one way they learn how to pray.

BOY:	Boy, I'd like to see that. But how do we resist him?
GIRL:	We just don't pay any attention to him. Don't listen to him. Don't talk to him.
BOY:	That means we don't give him the time of day. Right?
GIRL:	Right. I'd like to be part of God's army, too. But do I have to dress up like a soldier?
BOY:	No.
GIRL:	Oh, good. Giggles. I don't want to look like you.
BOY:	I don't want you to, either. Girls should look like girls and boys like boys! But you do need to wear the armor of God.
GIRL:	Armor of God? What's that?
BOY:	The helmet of salvation, the breastplate of righteousness, the belt of truth, the shield of faith, the sword of the Spirit, and the gospel of peace.
GIRL:	Scratches head. I don't know what you're talking about.
BOY:	I don't understand all about it either. But I do know that the Word of the Lord—the Bible—is our spiritual sword. When we obey God's Word, we have power to defeat the devil.
GIRL:	You mean, like obey the plan of salvation—repent, be baptized in Jesus' name, and receive the Holy Ghost?
BOY:	Right. That's how we start. Then just keep obeying God's Word.
GIRL:	That will make me a Christian soldier?
BOY:	Right.
GIRL:	Starts marching. Watch out, Satan. Here I come. Hup 1-2-3, hup 1-2-3 hup. . . .
BOY:	Marches with her as they exit. 1-2-3, hup 1-2-3, hup. . . .

Lead the children in singing, "I'm in the Lord's Army."
Make announcements, acknowledge birthdays, and greet visitors.
Play the review game, "Move Up" for a few minutes. Set a timer.

Warm Ups: Sing unto the Lord (5 minutes)

Since this is the last *POWer hour* in *The Winner's Series*, let the children choose their favorites from these lessons.
Allow time for two or three Dynamo Specials.

Knee Bends (3 minutes)

Move the pointer on the prayer spinner to one segment, *e.g.*, government leaders. Let the children name two or three people in government. After you have led in prayer for these leaders, move the pointer to the next segment. Continue praying for two or three people in each area.

Conclude by taking prayer requests from the children and leading them in congregational prayer.

Skit: Angels at Attention (4 minutes)

The angels follow the script from page 93.

Pushups (3 minutes)

This is the last *POWer hour* in *The Winner's Series*, and we are finishing on a note of victory. The *POWer line* is: When God is on our side, we are winners! If you are a winner, stand up and say this Christian soldier's cheer with me.

Angels at Attention

Enter angels. Beta is carrying camouflage clothes, a Bible, a shield, trumpet, etc. Binoculars hang around his neck. He places his clothing and weapons on a table or chair.

ALPHA: Smiling. **Don't tell me. You are a soldier?**

BETA: Shoulders back, salutes. **Yes. sir! At your command!**

ALPHA: **Who are you guarding now?**

BETA: Shoulders back, salutes. **Captain Gideon, sir.**

ALPHA: **Gideon? Oh, yes. Gideon is the man who mustered an army of 32,000 men.**

BETA: Shoulders back, salutes. **Yes, sir! But he didn't feed his men mustard.**

ALPHA: **Who said anything about mustard?**

BETA: **You did. You said, "He must-ard-ed an army of 32,000 men."**

ALPHA: **Some soldier you are. You don't even know army talk. I said, "He mustered an army." That means he got one together.**

BETA: Shoulders back, salutes. **Yes, sir! I understand, sir.**

ALPHA: **You don't have to salute me! I'm not your captain!**

BETA: Shoulders back, salutes. **Yes, sir! I mean, no, sir. I mean, I'm sorry, sir. Oh, I'm just trying to be a good soldier. And it takes practice.**

ALPHA: **That's true. We should all practice saying, "Yes, sir," and "No, sir." Isn't that right, kids?** Children should respond, "Yes, sir." If they do not, the angel reminds them to call him "sir." To Beta. **Who is Gideon's enemy?**

BETA: **The Midianites. They are some of the meanest and ugliest guys around.**

ALPHA: **Really?**

BETA: **They are out to destroy the Israelites.**

ALPHA: **How do they propose to do that? Kill them in battle?**

BETA: **No, they are trying to starve them to death. Every year after the Israelites have harvested their crops and stored their food for the winter, the Midianites steal it.**

ALPHA: **That is mean. It would be horrible to starve to death. I'd rather be shot.**

BETA: Whispers loudly. **The Midianites don't have guns. Remember, this is back in the days of swords and spears.**

ALPHA: **Oh, sorry about that. I'd rather have my head cut off than starve to death. If Israel will call on God, He will help them.**

BETA: **Oh, they have. That's why God sent Gideon.** Points to self proudly. **And me, of course.**

ALPHA: **Are you and Gideon doing your job?**

BETA: Looks embarrassed. **Well, I . . . I . . . I'm taking a little rest break. I'd better check and see how Gideon's doing.** Looks through binoculars. **Oh, no! They can't do that!**

ALPHA: **Do what?**

BETA: **A lot of Gideon's soldiers are checking out—leaving the army!**

ALPHA: **Why?**

BETA: **Shhhh. Be still so I can hear.** A few seconds silence. **I can't believe it. Gideon told everyone who was afraid to go home.**

ALPHA: **With God on their side what do they have to be afraid of?**

BETA: **Nothing. But I'm afraid they don't understand that. I'd better get down there right now and encourage Gideon.** Starts to leave.

ALPHA: **Wait. Aren't you forgetting something, soldier?**

BETA: Embarrassed. **Oh, yes. I forgot. Thank you.** Picks up clothes and weapons. Holds up Bible. **I especially need my sword! This defeats the enemy every time!**

ALPHA: Shoulders back, salutes. **Yes, sir!**

BETA: Shoulders back, salutes. **Reporting for duty, Captain Gideon.**
Beta exits. Alpha stands by the gate of heaven.

PERMISSION TO COPY SCRIPT

We find Gideon's story in the Book of Judges. Who can find Judges in their Bible? Let's see how many can find Judges in forty-three seconds. As soon as you find it, stand. Give all who are standing when time is called a round of applause.

V-I-C-T-O-R-Y
Victory, victory is our cry.
Are we winners?
Well I guess!
Christian soldiers. Yes! Yes! Yes!

Have the girls say the cheer, then the boys, then those on the left side of the room, those on the right side, etc. until everyone knows it.

Exercise: AIM (4 minutes)

Three-year-old LaVerne's family was moving. As they loaded the last of their belongings onto a horse-drawn carriage, little LaVerne scrambled into the front seat, holding a heavy black-bound book. It was her Papa's Bible. LaVerne knew this was a special book and must be handled with care.

Before she was born, God had told her Papa, "The child your wife is carrying will be mightily used of the Lord."

Little LaVerne loved God and the things of God. She played church with her paper dolls. When she was six, she was baptized.

As she grew, she wanted desperately to play the piano, but there was no money for lessons. So LaVerne and her mother quilted to pay for piano lessons.

When LaVerne was forty-one, she went to Liberia, West Africa as a missionary. On her forty-second birthday, her students gave her a surprise party. She received two pencils, a package of envelopes, a roll of film, seven nickels, one dime, one flower, three belts made of native material, one handbag, and one chicken. What a birthday party they had! No one knew this was her last birthday.

Seven months after she arrived in Liberia, Sister LaVerne Collins became ill and died. She had only been a missionary a few months, but she died happy, doing the will of the Lord. From the continent of Africa she walked through the gates of heaven and received her crown.

As the musician plays a march tune, such as, "Onward Christian Soldiers," let the children march to the beat and give their offering. Have you reached your offering goal? Give praise to the children and the Lord for the total whatever it is.

POWer of the Word

Beta should enter and take up his post beside the gate of heaven.

A Word from the Lord (4 minutes)

From the *kids POWer hour* tape play "A Word from the Lord" (hour 13).

All of the verses we heard on the tape are from the Book of Psalms. Can you find it in your Bible? Remember our biblical calisthenics. After the children have found the Book of Psalms, assign the verses to various groups, *e.g.*, "everyone wearing sneakers find Psalm 27 verse 3," "everyone wearing hard-soled shoes find Psalm 56 verse 4," "everyone not wearing shoes—oops, that won't work—everyone over twelve years old look up Psalm 113 verse 6."

Ask for each group to read their verse aloud. Briefly explain each verse after it has been read. Lead the children in a praise break, giving thanks for God's protecting power.

Training in the Word (4 minutes)

Ask everyone who can quote I John 5:4 to line up. Let them use the microphone. Give each one a pencil.

Ask a few questions to be sure they understand the meaning.

What does it mean to be "born of God"? How do we overcome the world? How does faith in God give us victory?

> *Spirit Generators:* Lead the children in a worship chorus to prepare their hearts for the Illustrated Sermon.

ILLUSTRATED SERMON

Gideon Wins the Battle (8 minutes)

Gideon and the angels use the script from page 96 to tell the Bible story.

Invitation and Prayer (5-? minutes)

Musician plays.

Who would have ever thought that God would use Gideon, a nobody, the baby of his family, a scaredy-cat, to win a mighty victory? God is not looking for big, brave people to do His work. He is looking for little people who know they can do nothing without God's help. God loves to take "nobodies" and make them into "somebodies." He loves to take "failures" and make them into "winners."

Tell the story of someone the children know and admire who came from humble beginnings and has done a great work for the Lord.

God wants to use you to defeat the devil. Are you willing to give your life to Jesus? Are you willing to say, "Whatever you want me to do, Jesus, I'll do it"? Whether you have received the Holy Ghost or not, raise your hand if you want to live for Jesus.

At this point, you may feel led to ask those with their hands raised to come forward for prayer. Or you may ask the trainers to move among the children and pray with them.

Review

Play again the move up game, starting with children who did not get to play at the beginning of the session.

Give each child a *POWer house* paper as he leaves.

Gideon Wins the Battle

Gideon enters and stands beside the sign pointing to heaven.

My name is Gideon and I am a farmer. I mean, I was a farmer before God called me into His army. After I left the army, I was a judge. You can see I had a pretty exciting life—farmer, soldier, judge. Which would you rather be?

One night when I was still a farmer, I was threshing wheat on my father's farm and I had this weird feeling that someone was watching me. When I turned to look, I couldn't believe my eyes. There stood an angel of the Lord!

He called me a "mighty man of valour." That means a brave soldier. I laughed. I was threshing wheat at night so the Midianites wouldn't see me, and I was hiding to do it! I wasn't brave at all; I was scared to death. Besides all that, I was the baby of my family. I was a little nobody—a coward!

The angel ignored all that and said God had called me to gather an army and defeat the Midianites. Remember, they are the guys who are stealing all our food? And there are so many of them that they couldn't be counted.

To my surprise when I asked for volunteers, thirty-two thousand men showed up. I was feeling pretty good. Maybe we could whip the Midianites after all. Then God said, "You've got too many soldiers. Send everyone home who is afraid." What? Send some home? We needed everyone we had.

God said, "I don't want you boasting in what you have done. I want you to know that whatever victory is won is won by My power, not yours."

When I told everyone who was afraid to go home, twenty-two thousand turned their backs and ran. How many soldiers did that leave me? I had thirty-two thousand and twenty-two thousand went home. Let the children figure it. **Right! I only had ten thousand left.**

Then God said, "You've still got too many." Man, I almost had a heart attack. The Midianite army had thousands and thousands, maybe hundreds of thousands of soldiers. I had ten thousand. And God said that was too many!

God told me to take the soldiers down to the river and tell them to get a drink. Those who scooped the water up in their hands and lapped it up with their tongue like a dog were to be separated from those who knelt down and put their faces in the water to drink. God said, "Keep the ones who lapped up the water with their tongue like a dog." Do you know why? They were on guard. The enemy could sneak up on the ones whose faces were in the water. God is sure smart! After the water test, I counted the soldiers left. I could hardly believe it. I had three hundred men. God expected me to fight the Midianites who couldn't be counted with three hundred men!

I was about to have a nervous breakdown, but God assured me that we would win. All I had to do was obey His orders.

I gave each man a trumpet, an empty pitcher, and a torch. Strange weapons, huh? It wasn't the weapons that were going to give us victory. It was God. I told the soldiers to watch and listen closely, and do what I did.

When all was dark and still, we surrounded the camp of the enemy. Our lighted torches were inside our pitchers so not even a glimmer of light shown. In one hand each soldier held a pitcher and torch. In the other hand he held a trumpet. It was pitch dark and silent.

Suddenly, I broke my pitcher. The torch flared brilliantly. I blew my trumpet and cried, "The sword of the Lord and of Gideon." Three hundred men did the same thing. You should have heard it! You should have seen it!

The dark night came to life as lights blazed all around the camp of the Midianites. And the noise! It sounded like a mighty army!

The sleeping soldiers awoke with thumping hearts and weak knees. Crazy with fear, they grabbed their swords and started swinging, killing one another. It was wild! We Israelites just stood our ground and watched as the enemy destroyed each other.

Praise God. What a victory! No matter how small and insignificant you are, when God is on your side, you are a winner!

Angels step toward Gideon as music plays.

BETA: Blows the trumpet. **Hear ye! Hear ye! Gideon, mighty man of God, step forward to receive your reward.**
Gideon moves forward to meet the angels.

ALPHA: Reads from scroll. **Gideon, youngest son of Joash, servant of the living God, and mighty warrior, welcome to the gates of heaven. Everyone stand, please.**
You were small and insignificant but because you were obedient to God, you became a mighty leader. You overcame fear and obeyed orders! Great is your reward. Presents Gideon with a crown/trophy.
Enter into the joys of the Lord.

Gideon enters into heaven and the gate is closed behind him.

PERMISSION TO COPY SCRIPT

take home paper ages 4–6

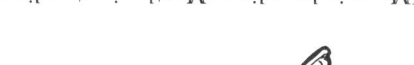

A POWer house 1

At God's House

Mary and Martha were Jesus' friends. Mary loved to sit at Jesus' feet and listen to Him. Once she anointed Jesus' feet with perfume. Her sister, Martha, was always busy serving Jesus. ✏️ Color these pictures of Mary and Martha. How do you know which one is Mary and which one is Martha? ✂️ Cut out the box of ointment and put it in Mary's hands. ✂️ Cut out the serving tray and put it in Martha's.

(Mary is kneeling, Martha is standing.)

At Your House

✝ Jesus is a friend who will never forsake us.

Dear Parent,

At kids POWer hour, we started "The Winner's Series." In the first unit, "A Winning Team," our aim is to help your child develop a relationship with Jesus Christ. We studied today about "My Best Friend."

Jesus has promised that He "will never leave us or forsake us." That's comforting for both children and adults.

The story has been told of the man who wanted to convince a child that there was no God. He posted a sign, "God is nowhere." He asked the child, "What does that sign say?" The trusting child responded, "God is now here."

To help reinforce the truths we learned at kids POWer hour, would you work these activities into your schedule?

✓ Vote on it. Who is your family's best friend—other than Jesus? Take a secret ballot.
✓ Do it. Have Friend's Day at your house. Invite this special family friend to dinner.
✓ Play it. How many friends does your family have? Set a timer for one minute. How many friends can your family name in that minute? When time is called, take another minute to give thanks for your friends.

We thank God for all of you, our friends.

kids POWer hour staff

Permission to photocopy this page granted for church use.

At God's House

How sharp are you feeling? Who is who in these pictures? Draw a line from the name to the person.

Mary

Martha

Lazarus

At Your House

Powerhouse 1

Jesus is a friend who will never forsake us.

✏️ Write each of these phrases on a piece of paper.

(1) I will never leave thee, nor forsake thee.

(2) So that we may boldly say, The Lord is my helper.

(3) And I will not fear what man shall do unto me.

Do you remember where this is found in your Bible? (The answer is upside down on the bottom of this page.)

Put these papers around your house where you will see them often. How about on the bathroom mirror or your bedroom door? They will be good reminders of your Best Friend's promise to be with you. This promise is for your family, too.

Put your mission bank on a table where it will be seen often by your family. Ask your parents to drop in their change (and do the same yourself). And while you are giving to missions, remember to pray for the missionaries, too.

You have never seen a picture of this family. How did you recognize—

Mary?

Martha?

Lazarus?

Hebrews 13:5-6

take home paper ages 4-6

Permission to photocopy this page granted for church use.

At God's House

POWer house 2

At Your House

✂ Cut out the sheep face. Cut out the ears. Position the ears behind the head as shown. Cut on the line break above the mouth (this separates the mouth for the paper sack). Glue both pieces onto a paper lunch sack, as shown. Glue on cotton balls for a "wool" effect.

♪ **The Good Shepherd provides for and protects His sheep.**

Dear Parent,

Please help your "little lamb" make a paper plate puppet. Encourage him to use it to teach you a song he has learned in kids POWer hour. Perhaps he will also tell you about David the shepherd boy.

Thanks for sharing your child with us.

kids POWer hour staff

EAR

EAR

CUT

Make a paper sack puppet to remind you that you are Jesus' lamb. He will take care of you.

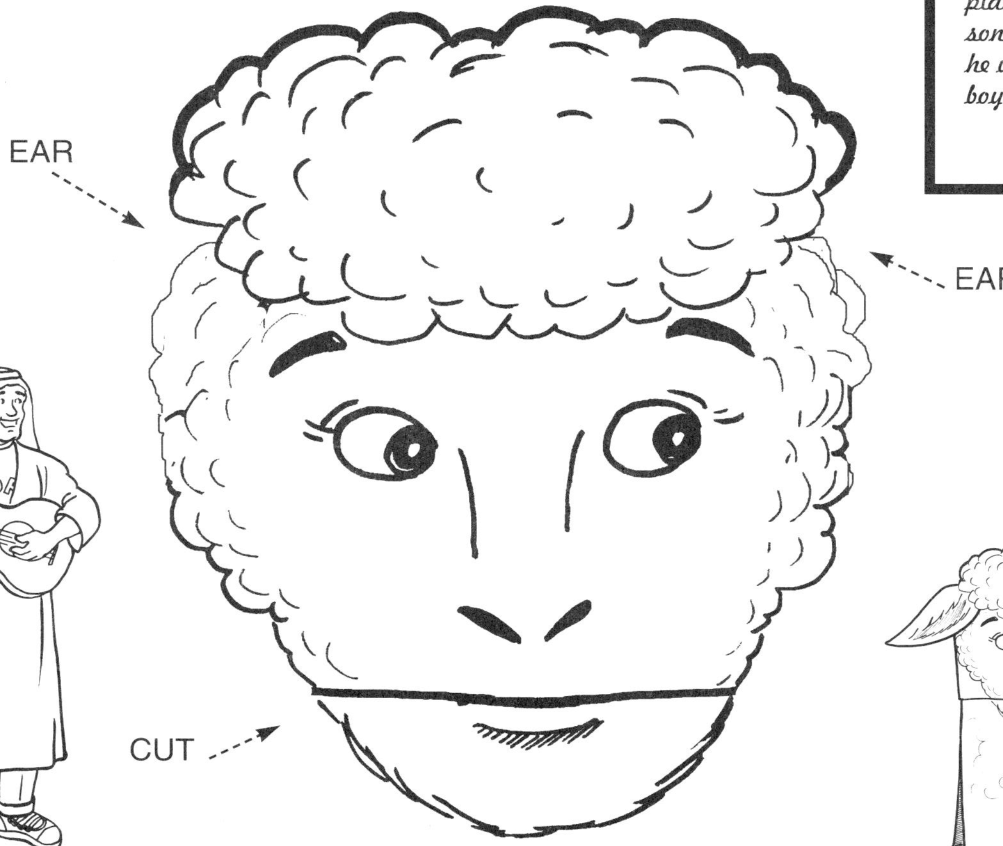

Powerhouse 2

At God's House

✏️ We studied about the Good Shepherd who gave His life for His sheep. The Good Shepherd is _____. The sheep are _____. Another shepherd who watches over us is our _____.

✏️ Copy the sketches from the art bank to fill in the picture frames.

"I am the good _____: the good shepherd giveth his life for the _____.

But he that is an hireling, and not the shepherd, whose own the sheep are not, seeth the _____ coming, and leaveth the sheep, and fleeth:

I am the good shepherd, and know my sheep, and am known of mine" (John 10:11-12, 14).

At Your House

The Good Shepherd provides for and protects His sheep.

✈️ Make a paper sack puppet. Use it to teach a song you learned in kids POWer hour and tell the story of David the shepherd boy to a small friend.

✏️ Draw a sheep face onto a paper lunch sack. Be sure to split the head as shown so that the mouth will separate when you use your puppet.

Cover the sheep with cotton balls to make a "wool" effect. The ears could be made out of strong white paper towels, or white construction paper.

take home paper ages 4-6

Permission to photocopy this page granted for church use.

At God's House

POWer hour

B

This poor woman had been bent over for eighteen years. Then Jesus touched her and she could stand straight.

✂ Cut out the woman. Use paper brads to put her together so she can bend over and stand straight.

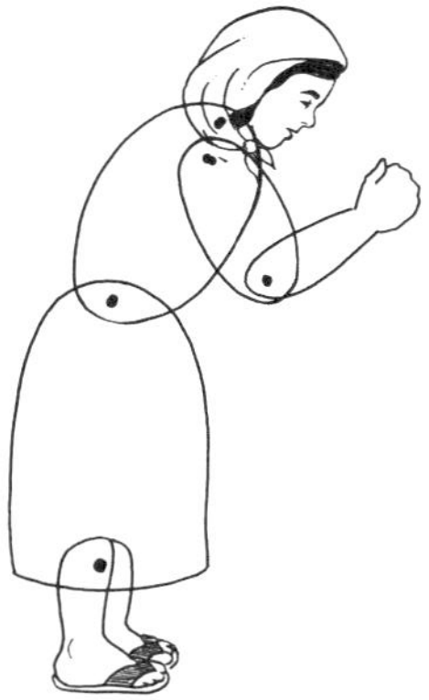

At Your House

Jesus heals emotional as well as physical pain.

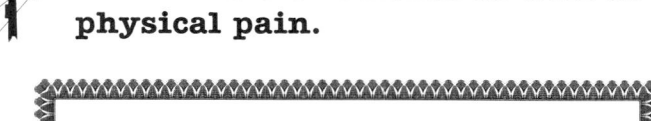

Dear Parent,

Imagine being able to meet someone's gaze, to look up at the stars, to straighten your shoulders after years of looking at the ground. That's what happens when Jesus touches us. He lifts our vision beyond the dirt and helps us walk straight and tall.

In kids POWer hour we learned that Jesus heals hurt feelings and the pain inside which makes us cry, as well as the "ouchie" on our knee.

If trouble and pain has bent you double inside, let Jesus touch you.

✓ When your child is hurting (whether physically or emotionally), pray with him. Jesus touches children, too.

✓ Talk to your child about the things which hurt him and the things which he might do which would hurt others.

We are praying for your family and would appreciate your prayers for our children's church.

kids POWer hour staff

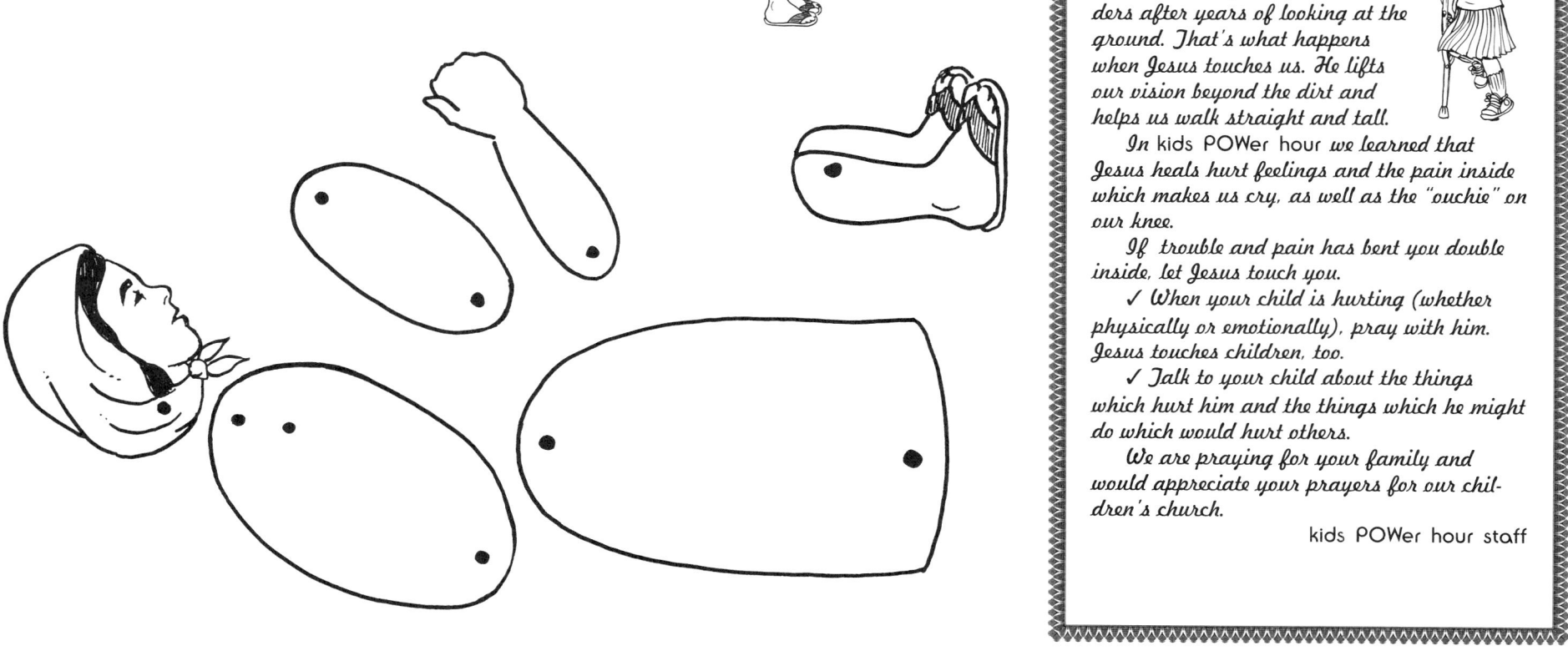

At God's House

In the word bank are pictures of the missing words. Draw a line from the art to the space where it goes to complete the word and make a rebus puzzle.

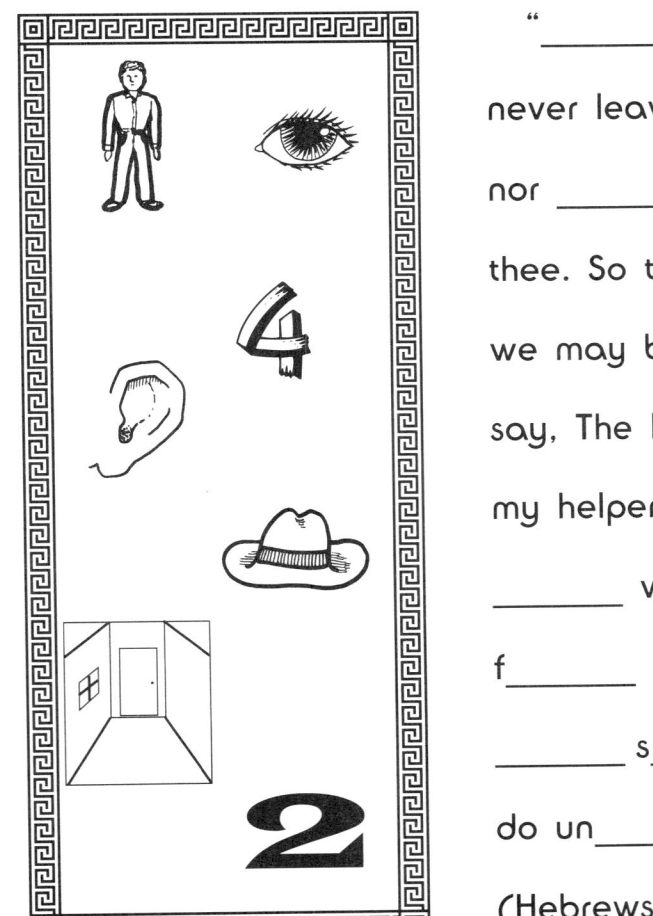

"_____ will never leave thee, nor _____ sake thee. So t_____ we may boldly say, The Lord is my helper, and _____ will not f_____ what s_____ do un_____ me" (Hebrews 13:5-6).

Powerhouse B

At Your House

Jesus heals emotional as well as physical pain.

Do your spiritual exercises every day.

✓ First, do your warm-ups. On a piece of paper write in big letters, "SING." Tape this to the wall at the foot of your bed so it is the first thing you see when you wake up. Get up singing.

✓ Morning and evening do knee bends. Pray as you start the day and before you go to bed.

✓ Then do your pushups. Push yourself up by lifting up Jesus. Every day talk to someone about Jesus. You do not have to say a lot, but say something.

take home paper ages 4-6

At God's House

My POWer house

At Your House

✏️ Color these hearts like the hearts in your mini-songbook, "My Heart was Black as Sin."
✂️ Cut them out and ask an adult to help you put them together with yarn.

✝️ Jesus came to save us from our sins.

Dear Parent,

In kids POWer hour we studied about the Samaritan woman at the well who was a loser—a big time loser—until she met Jesus. Then she became a winner—a soul winner.

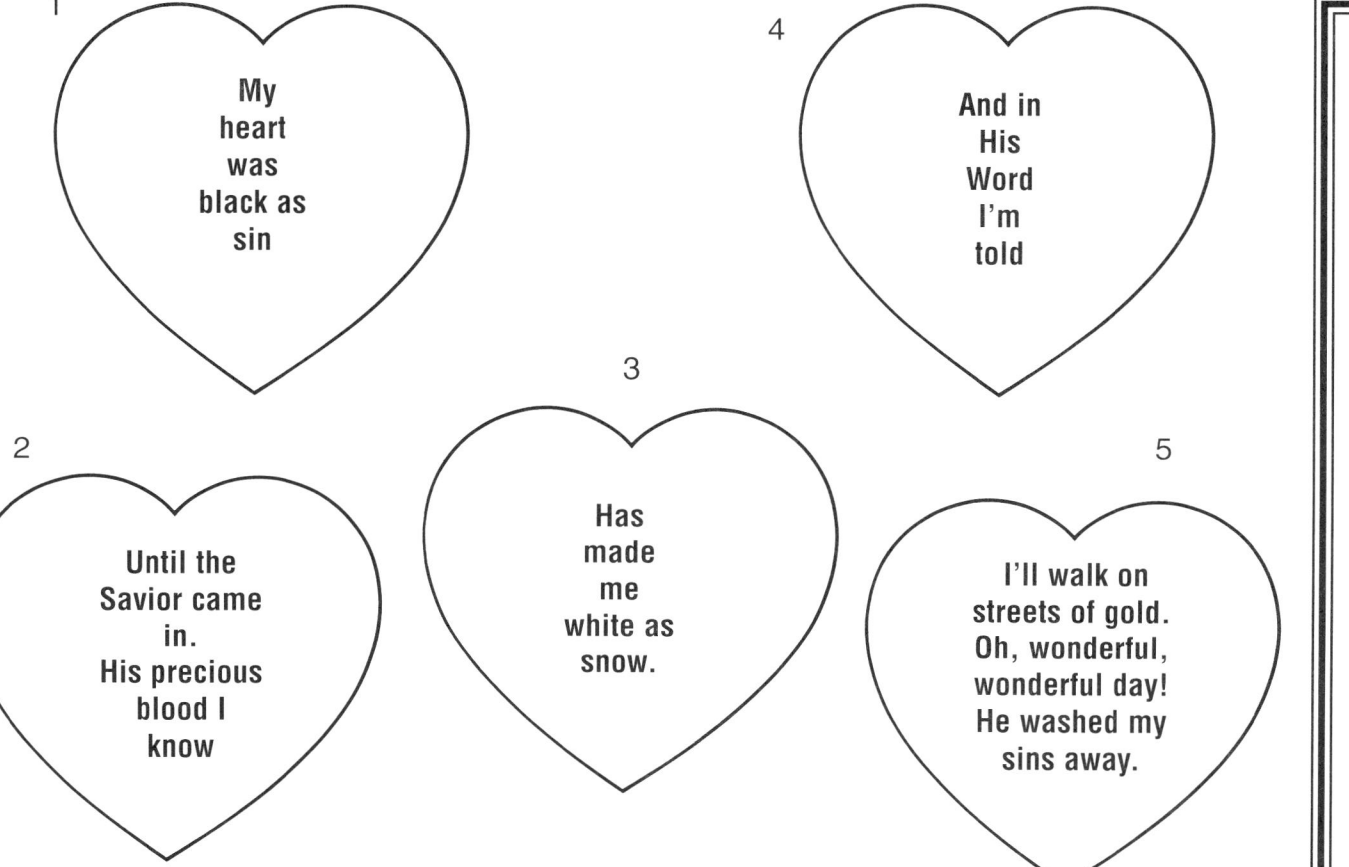

We learned that Jesus came to save us from our sins. The story of Rusty and Bud should have helped your child understand the concept of a Savior.

✓ Talk about it. Ask your child to tell you the story about the dogs. Relate it to how Jesus saves us from sin.

✓ Sing it. Ask your child to teach you the song, "My Heart Was Black as Sin," using his mini-songbook.

✓ Remind your child he is a winner!

Thanks for working with us to reinforce the things your child hears at kids POWer hour.

kids POWer hour staff

1. My heart was black as sin

2. Until the Savior came in. His precious blood I know

3. Has made me white as snow.

4. And in His Word I'm told

5. I'll walk on streets of gold. Oh, wonderful, wonderful day! He washed my sins away.

Give this mini-songbook to a friend.

1-black   2-red   3-white   4-brown   5-gold or yellow

Permission to photocopy this page granted for church use.

take home paper ages 7-11

At God's House

We learned some new words for "water." Can you match each word to the correct language?

1. wasser
2. agua
3. pani
4. mizu
5. l'eau
6. tubig
7. voda

A. Russian
B. Urdu (Pakistan)
C. Japanese
D. Spanish
E. Tagalog (Philippines)
F. German
G. French

What is living water?

Uhhh . . . uhhh . . . it's . . . uhhh . . . it's water that is alive.

A good guess, but not good enough. Kids, tell him what living water is.

Powerhouse 4

Jesus came to save us from our sins.

Meeting Jesus changed the Samaritan woman from a loser to a winner—a soul winner. You do not have to be a preacher to be a soul winner. You can do what the Samaritan woman did. You can invite people to meet Jesus. You do this by inviting them to church.

✏ Write on this notepad the names of three people you will invite to church this week.

At Your House

I am a winner

Hold this important message up to a mirror.

Answers: 1-F, 2-D, 3-B, 4-C, 5-G, 6-E, 7-A

Permission to photocopy this page granted for church use.

POWer house

At God's House

✂ Cut out the baby Moses and place him in the picture wherever you want him.

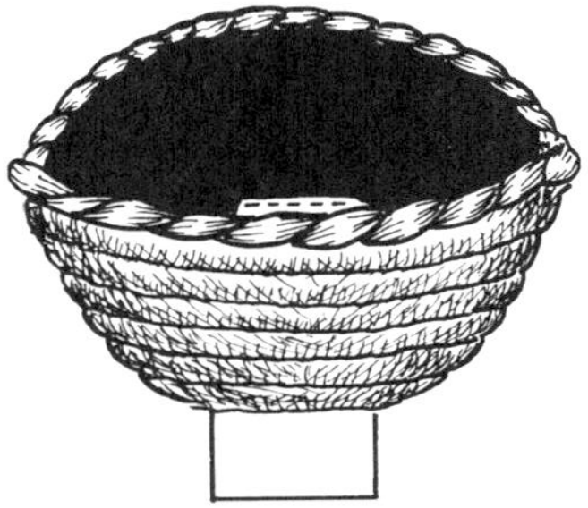

take home paper ages 4-6

Permission to photocopy this page granted for church use.

At Your House

5 _____

▸ Every child is a gifted and talented child.

Dear Parent,

We learned in kids POWer hour that every child has been given gifts by God. One of the many awesome responsibilities given parents is discovering their child's gifts.

Often the characteristic in your child which annoys you the most is actually a trait of his gift. The child who wants to keep every stray cat and dog may well have the gift of compassion. The child who bosses everyone and asks a thousand "why's?" a day may have the gift of administration.

One translation of Proverbs 22:6, "Train up a child in the way he should go," is "Train a child for his proper trade, and he will never leave it, even when he is old." Many adults spend a lifetime looking for their niche in life because when they were young they were not properly directed.

This week watch for your child's gifts and encourage him to use them—even if you have to take in a stray cat!

God bless you and your family—and your pets.

kids POWer hour staff

take home paper ages 7-11

At God's House

Powerhouse 5

Every child is a gifted and talented child.

We learned that God has given every child gifts. Miriam had several gifts. ✏️ Work this rebus to discover two of her gifts.

We also learned that it is not bragging to recognize our gifts. On these gifts, write three things that you like to do and are good at doing.

At Your House

God wants you to use your gifts to help others, just as Miriam used hers to help her brother, Moses.

Hmmm. I love motors. I could mow the lawn for old Mr. Carson.

Make an agreement with yourself to wisely use your gifts this week.

My Agreement with Myself

I do hereby promise myself that I will use my gift of _____ to help _____ by _____ this week.

Signed: _____
Date: _____

Permission to photocopy this page granted for church use.

take home paper ages 4-6

Permission to photocopy this page granted for church use.

At God's House

⇨ Practice drawing David and Goliath using these simple steps.

At Your House

God gives us gifts, but we must practice to develop them.

Dear Parent,

Are you familiar with the slogan, "citius, altius, fortius"? It is the Olympic motto, which translates, "Swifter, higher, stronger." Brutus Hamilton, coach of the U.S. Olympic team several years ago, decided there had to be limits to human speed, strength, agility, and endurance. So he compiled a list of what he considered to be the "ultimate" in track and field performances. Since then, every one of these limits has been broken.

At kids POWer hour we are teaching your child that he "can do all things through Christ which strengthens him." You can help instill this message in him.

✓ *Praise him. Any time your child does a job, praise what he has done. If when coloring, he got out of line fifteen times and stayed in once, praise the one time.*

✓ *Encourage him to stretch himself. Say, "Sure you can do it. Go for it." Little David slew the giant while his big brothers trembled in fear. There is no telling what your little one can do with confidence in God and himself.*

We believe in your child.

       kids POWer hour staff

At God's House

What does "citius, altius, fortius," mean?

That's a good guess, but not exactly right. What does it mean, kids? Write your answer on this notepad.

Uhhh, something about . . . uhhhh, something about beating your own record.

Answers: faster, higher, braver or swifter, higher, stronger

Powerhouse

God gives us gifts, but we must practice to develop them.

What's your talent? ✔ Check the things you can do.

- ☐ play a musical instrument
- ☐ draw
- ☐ care for the elderly
- ☐ memorize God's Word
- ☐ witness
- ☐ cook
- ☐ sing
- ☐ write
- ☐ baby sit
- ☐ fix things
- ☐ yard work
- ☐ other: _____

What can you do to improve your talents? Make up a practice plan for the coming week. Write what you will do each day.

Monday:
Tuesday:
Wednesday:
Thursday:
Friday:

At Your House

At God's House

POWerhouse 7

At Your House

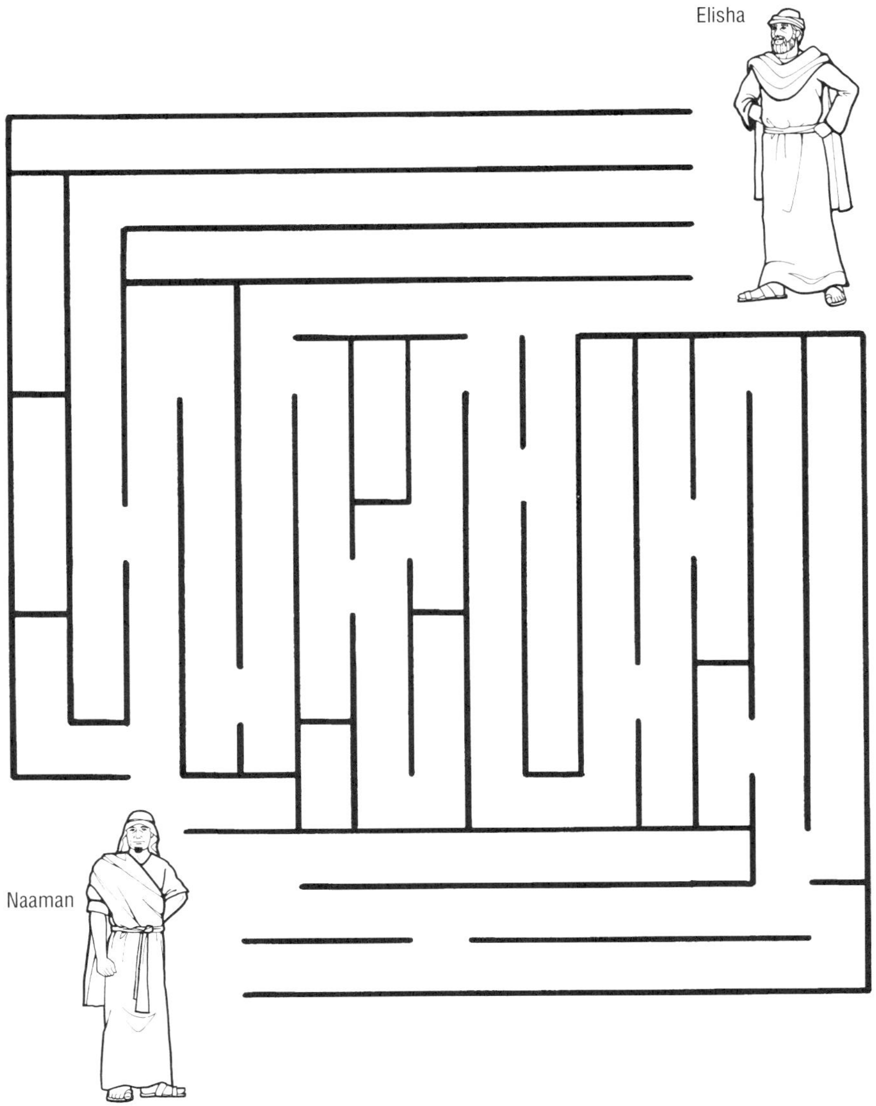

No matter what our circumstances we can be a powerful witness for the Lord.

Dear Parent,

At kids POWer hour we are placing a special emphasis on missions in this series. Today we studied about a little maid who was a witness in a foreign land.

✓ Ask your child to say for you the mission cheer he learned at kids POWer hour.

✓ At bedtime instead of telling your child a story, ask him to tell you the story of "Naaman's Maid, the Powerful Witness."

✓ Are you a mission-minded family? Children learn best by example. If you want your child to live by God's principle of giving, let him see you give to missions. And why not give him extra duties and pay him with "mission points" which he can exchange for cash to give in the kids POWer hour mission offering? We have an exciting project which we are giving to. Ask him to tell you about it—if he hasn't already (a dozen times).

May God bless you and your family.

— kids POWer hour staff

Elisha

Naaman

The little maid in our Bible story told her master about the prophet in her homeland. Naaman went to the prophet Elisha and was healed. ➡ Help Naaman find his way to the prophet.

At God's House

We learned about a slogan which fits Christians as well as runners in the Olympics.

📖 To refresh your memory, decode this puzzle.

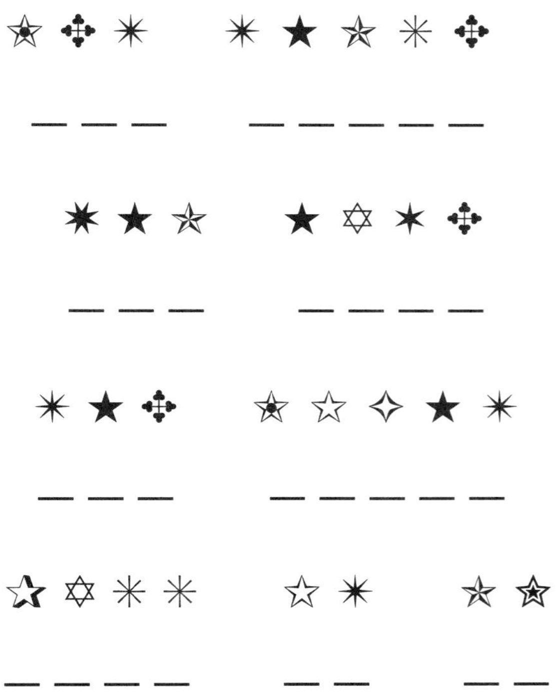

✥ ✻ — — ✻ ✶ ✥

✶ ★ ✩ — — — ✶ ✻ ✥

✻ ✶ ✥ — — ★ ✩ ✻ ★ ✥ ★

✩ ✻ ✶ — ✩ ✻ ✶ ✩ ✻ ✩

CODE

✩ A	✥ E	✶ G	★ H	✻ I
★ L	✶ N	✩ O	✩ P	✻ S
✻ T	★ V	✻ W		

Powerhouse 7

✦ **No matter what our circumstances we can be a powerful witness for the Lord.**

At Your House

You can pass the Word of the Lord on to other members of your family.

✓ Ask your parents, brothers, and sisters if they know Philippians 4:13. (You could even ask your grandparents.) If they do not, teach it to them. That's one way to pass on the torch.

✓ At bedtime volunteer to tell a story to your little brother or sister, if you are blessed enough to have one. Then tell the story of "Naaman's Maid, the Powerful Witness."

✓ Do you keep a diary? If not, start today. You do not have to have a fancy diary. A notebook of any kind will do. Each day copy a verse from the Bible in your diary and memorize it.

✓ Create a code like the one on this paper. Using your code, write the name of a person you want to see come to the Lord on a slip of paper. Pin this to your pillow or put it on your mirror. Every day pray for this person, and when you get a chance, witness to him.

What can a child do for the Lord? Turn this word around to find out.

STOL

At God's House

We learned about serving others. ➡ Color these pictures. ◯ Then draw a circle around the children which are helping someone.

They are all helpers, aren't they? You can be a helper, too. Ask your mother or dad what you can do to help.

kids POWer hour 8

At Your House

✝ **Before we can be served, we must learn to serve.**

Dear Parent,

kids POWer hour is training ground for the leaders of tomorrow. Today we learned that before we can lead or be served, we must learn to follow or serve.

We also learned another word for "servant." It is "minister." Many people are wanting a ministry. Few realize that serving is a ministry. To prepare your child for a bright future as a "minister," teach him to serve. Here's a fun activity to teach him, and get some jobs done around the house.

✓ Play it. This game is for everyone in the family big enough to walk and talk. Before starting, give several options of what the reward could be — a trip to the ice cream store, a picnic, a hike, etc. On slips of paper write simple jobs that need to be done around the house. (Break big jobs up into little bites.) Place in a box. Beside it put a sheet of paper with the players' names. Each player draws a slip and runs to do his job. When a job is finished, another player must "inspect and okay" it. The inspector then puts a mark beside the door's name on the paper. The player draws another slip and starts over. When all the jobs are done, celebrate. Let the player with the most points decide what the celebration will be. Have fun!

kids POWer hour staff

take home paper ages 4-6

Permission to photocopy this page granted for church use.

At God's House

Hidden in this paragraph is the title of an important person in the church.
Read this story and find the letters which are different. ✏ Write them on the line below.

Elisha, Elijah's servant, was like the prophet's **S**hadow. He followed him everywhere h**E** went. As Elisha served, he lea**R**ned everything he could from Elijah. Elisha knew that someday Elijah would be gone, and he would ha**V**e to do his job. Then it happened! One day Elijah was caught up to heaven in **A** whirlwind. Because Elisha had been a good serva**N**t, Elijah left him his mantle, his position, and a double por**T**ion of his power.

_ _ _ _ _ _ _

Do you have trouble remembering who came first, Elijah or Elisha?

Here's a memory trick to help you.

Both start with "Eli."

Then which comes first, "j" or "s"?

So **Eli**jah comes before **Eli**sha.

Powerhouse

At Your House

✝ Before we can be served, we must learn to serve.

Here's a badge for you to wear. Oops! Can't do that! Then everyone would know you are the "secret servant."

You can wear it inside your clothes. Pin it inside against your shirt. When you feel it against your skin, it will remind you to serve. ✏ Fill it out. ✂ Cut it out. Pin it in. And get to work. You are about to have the time of your life, surprising people and keeping them guessing!

At your house you can be a servant.

Oh, yuk! Who wants to be a servant?

I do. I want to be a secret servant. It's fun!

You can be a secret servant, too. What can you do this week to serve others in secret?

Secret Servant

name _____

At God's House

POWer house

Moses could not talk plain, but he still did wonderful things for God.
- Color these pictures.
- Then cut them out and use them to tell the story of Moses to a friend.

At Your House

Whatever our disabilities, we can succeed.

Dear Parent,

At kids POWer hour we talked about disabilities. We learned that everyone has a disability of some kind. But, no matter what our disability, we can succeed.

✓ Talk about it. Ask your child to tell you the story of Mae Ivy, the missionary to China. Talk about people you know with disabilities who have succeeded.

✓ Remember it. At the table after you say grace, repeat together Philippians 4:13: "I can do all things through Christ which strengtheneth me." This verse will help your child succeed in life. Help him remember it. It is also a good one for parents.

✓ Do it. Take your child to visit a disabled person who is at ease talking about his disability. Help your child become comfortable around people who are in wheelchairs, blind, or disabled in other ways.

Thanks for sharing your child with us at kids POWer hour.

kids POWer hour staff

take home paper ages 4-6

Permission to photocopy this page granted for church use.

take home paper ages 7-11

At God's House

Powerhouse

Here is something we can all do if we will obey Jesus. To find what it is, work this puzzle. The word on the top line is the answer.

Is there something you can't do?

I can't see very well without my glasses.

And I can't even draw a straight stick man.

COACH

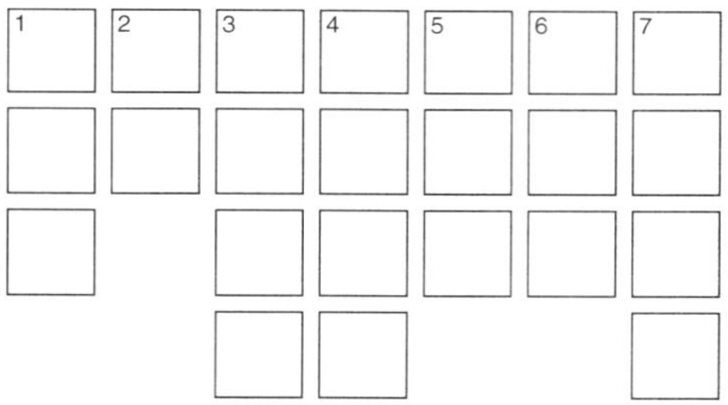

Down:
1. Rises in the east
2. Opposite of down
3. Hates dogs
4. You wear it in cold weather.
5. You do this at dinner time.
6. You hear with this.
7. Hates cats

Whatever our disabilities, we can succeed.

Do you know others who are disabled? Perhaps they are blind, crippled, deaf, or have trouble reading or doing math? Even though you have a disability (and we all do), you can do something to help someone who needs you.

✂ Color in the segments on this clock to show how much time you will give this week to helping someone.

✂ As a reminder, cut it out and put it on the wall or a mirror in your room.

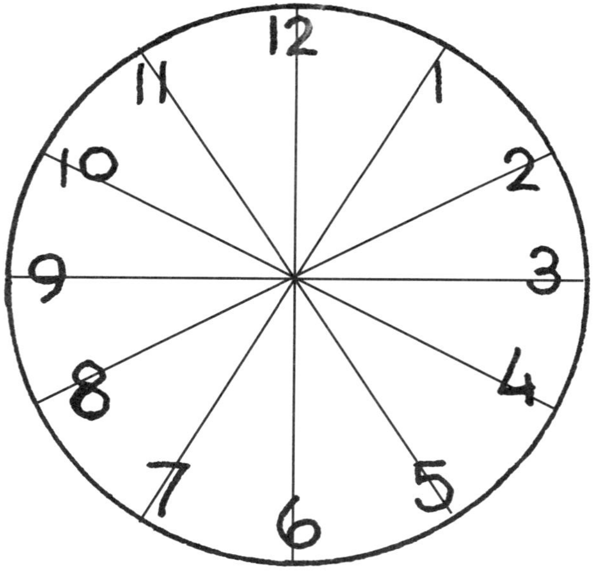

At Your House

Permission to photocopy this page granted for church use.

At God's House

POWer house 10

Joseph's father gave him a special coat made of many colors. Color this coat by number.

1 = black   2 = green   3 = blue   4 = red   5 = silver   6 = gold

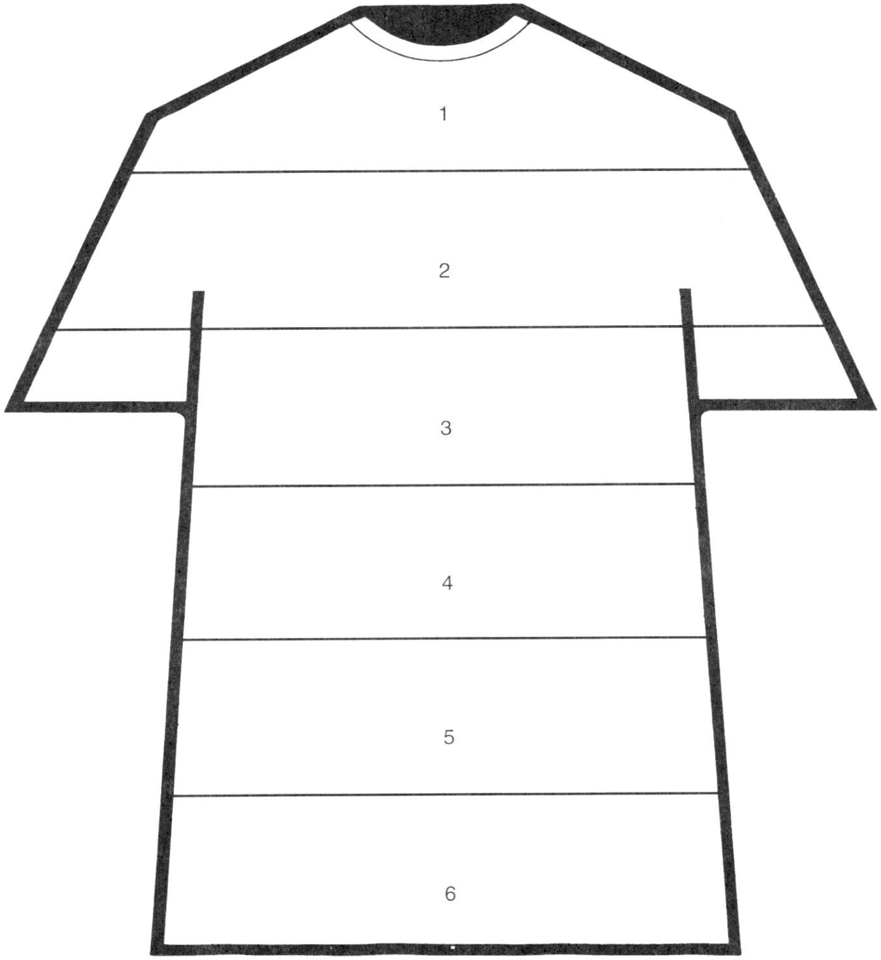

At Your House

A right attitude can make rejection bearable and eventually turn it into acceptance.

Dear Parent,

At sometime, everyone suffers rejection. And we never get so old, but what it hurts. Children are especially vulnerable to rejection, whether by peers, family, or strangers. Rejection is an obstacle that we must hurdle or it will crush us.

We know that you, as a parent, are doing everything you can to assure that your child feels accepted and loved at home. Here are a couple of suggestions which might help.

✓ Talk about it. At the dinner table ask each member to name two foods which they love and two which they dislike. Discuss how the broccoli Jodi thinks is "yucky," Mom loves. As Jodi grows her tastes will change and someday she may decide broccoli is "yummy." Apply this to how people accept or reject others. While we should not reject someone simply because they don't suit our "taste," it is a fact that it often happens. It has nothing to do with our value as a person.

✓ Do it. When your child is going through a difficult time, have a "Jodi" day. Fix her favorite food, free her from all "duties," hug her everytime she passes you. Let her be "queen for a day" at your house. Talk about her good qualities.

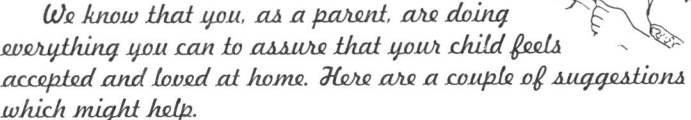

At kids POWer hour your child is accepted and loved.

kids POWer hour staff

---

take home paper ages 4-6

Permission to photocopy this page granted for church use.

take home paper ages 7-11

At God's House

✏️ Write your response in the empty balloon.

"You're not invited to my party because your parents do not live on our side of town."

"You can't join our club because you're too goody-goody."

Powerhouse 10 ①

✝️ **A right attitude can make rejection bearable and eventually turn it into acceptance.**

✏️ ✂️ Color and cut out these stickers. To make the "sticky," mix equal parts of Elmer's® glue and water. Brush on the back of the stickers. Turn them upside down and leave until they are dry. To stick on, simply moisten the back.

You're tops.

You're a star.

You're an angel.

Give these stickers to a friend to let them know they are accepted and loved by you.

At Your House

Permission to photocopy this page granted for church use.

At God's House

POWer house 11

At Your House

A stand for right brings great rewards.

Daniel and his friends stood for right.

✂ Cut out these feet. Glue to a square of posterboard. Cut posterboard in shape of feet. Blow up your balloon. Tie it. Slip the knot through the slit between the feet. Now your balloon man can stand for right.

Dear Parent,

At kids POWer hour we learned how Daniel and his three friends took a stand for right in refusing to eat the king's meat and drink his wine.

To help your child understand the concept of "standing for right," we suggest the following:

✓ Talk about it. At the dinner table, talk about why various foods are good for you, while others are not. Tell about a time when you were a child and you ate too much chocolate candy (or junk food) and it made you sick.

✓ Do role plays. Act out simple scenarios which your child might face in the future. Write on slips of paper possible temptations, such as, puff on a cigarette, tell a lie, steal, play with matches. Add some positive scenarios also—feed a pet, pick up toys, share with a friend. Talk about the consequences of each action.

✓ Do it. Reinforce good behavior, making sure your child understands why he is being rewarded.

Your child is special to us.

kids POWer hour staff

take home paper ages 7-11

At God's House

We learned how Daniel and his friends were rewarded for taking a stand for right. How much of the Bible story do you remember? If the statement is true, circle the letter in the true column. If it is false, circle the letter in the false column. Then write the circled letters on the lines below to find the mystery word.

	True	False
1. Daniel was a prisoner-of-war in Babylon.	L	M
2. Daniel had four friends who stood with him.	C	O
3. Daniel would not eat the king's food because he did not like it.	X	V
4. Daniel asked for a diet of vegetables and water.	E	B
5. Daniel and his friends were given positions of honor in Babylon.	D	A

Daniel and his friends stood for right because they ___ ___ ___ God.

Powerhouse 11

A stand for right brings great rewards.

Daniel and his friends stood for right.
✂ Cut out these feet. Glue to a square of posterboard. Cut posterboard in shape of feet. Blow up your balloon. Tie it. Slip the knot through the slit between the feet.
Now your balloon can stand for right.
✏ With a felt marker, very carefully draw a face on your balloon man.

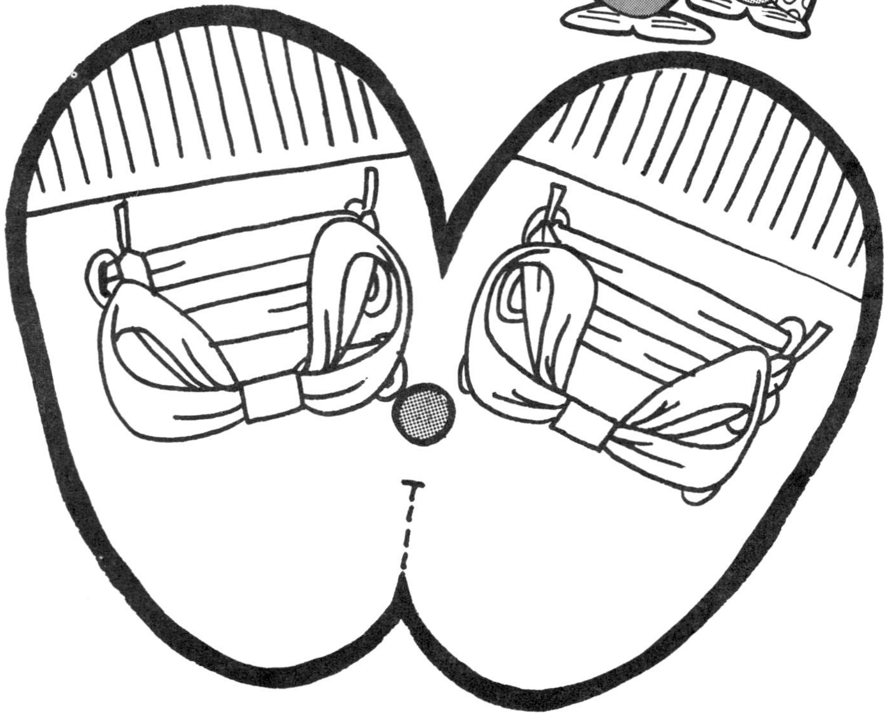

At Your House

Permission to photocopy this page granted for church use.

At God's House

POWerhouse 12

At Your House

Courage is fear that has said its prayers.

Queen Esther did a very brave thing when she went before the king. Connect the dotted lines to finish this picture. Then color it. Can you tell this story to a friend?

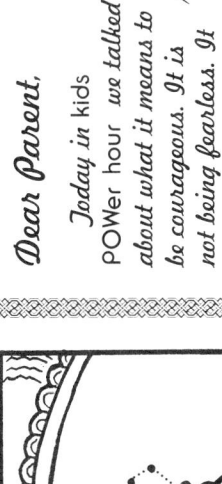

Dear Parent,

Today in kids POWer hour we talked about what it means to be courageous. It is not being fearless. It is doing what has to be done in spite of fear.

Everyone is afraid of something. But fear, when it joins hands with prayer, becomes courage.

✓ Try it. When your child is afraid, pray with him.

✓ Talk about it. Tell your child what you fear (as long as it is something that will not cause fear in the child). Ask your child to pray for you. This will encourage him to tell you his fears.

✓ Do it. Have a balloon release. Purchase one helium balloon for each family member. Each names his fear and writes it on a slip of paper. After everyone attaches his paper to his balloon string, lead the family in a simple prayer, releasing the fear. Then let it go! Your child will never forget this beautiful way of releasing fear.

kids POWer hour staff

---

take home paper ages 4-6

Permission to photocopy this page granted for church use.

At God's House

Are you learning the books of the Bible? Complete this dot-to-dot starting with Genesis and ending with II Kings. If you need help, use the table of contents in your Bible.

"Queen Esther sure was brave."

"Yes, but she was also very scared."

"That's what being brave is. Doing what you need to do even though you are afraid."

- II Samuel
- I Samuel
- Ruth
- Judges
- Joshua
- Deuteronomy
- Numbers
- Leviticus
- Exodus
- Genesis
- II Kings
- I Kings

Powerhouse 12

Courage is fear that has said its prayers.

Think about this. Have you ever done something you were afraid to do? Like ride a roller coaster? Or give a book report in front of your class? Or go to the altar in front of everyone? Or apologize to a friend? How did you feel after you overcame your fear?

Is there something you need to do, but are scared to do? Make a note of it on this pad. Then cut it out and give it to an adult you trust. Ask them to help you pray that you can overcome your fear.

When you overcome your fear and do what you need to do, be sure to tell that friend and thank him for his prayers.

At Your House

kids POWer hour 13

If God is on our side, we are winners.

At God's House

Cut out the trophy. Have an adult help you cut slits on the dotted lines. Slip the top of a pencil through the slits to make a pencil topper.

Gideon was a winner. And you are, too, if you are on God's side.

At Your House

You have just completed *The Winner's Series*—and that makes you a Winner! Cut out the ribbon below and let everyone know that you are a winner for Jesus!

You are a Winner!

Dear Parent,

The past thirteen POWer hours we have emphasized over and over that your child is a "winner"—not because he is smart or good-looking (which, of course, he is), but because he is on the Lord's team.

Gideon was the baby of his family and scared half to death of the Midianites. Yet the angel of the Lord called him "a mighty man of valour"—which he discovered he was when he said, "Yes," to God. God delights in making "somebodies" out of "nobodies." He loves to do "much" with "little."

✓ Talk about it. What makes a winner? Is it the highest score or the fastest runner? Emphasize that anyone who does his best is a "winner" even if he is the last one to cross the finish line.

✓ Reward your child for jobs well done by giving him a pat on the back, a bear hug, and/or words of praise.

You can be proud of your child. He is a winner!

kids POWer hour staff

take home paper ages 7-11

At God's House

Powerhouse 1B

At Your House

If God is on our side, we are winners.

Cut out the trophy. Have an adult help you cut slits on the dotted lines. Slip the top of a pencil through the slits to make a pencil topper. You might want to give this winner's pencil to a friend or family member who is feeling blue.

Find the hidden message. Starting with the first letter, write every other letter in the spaces below.

Gboedelaolvpex
sctwokmhalkneq
szotmieabmoed
wiaexsuowubteo
xfbnqoebpordy
ipeos.

_____ _____ _____
_____ _____ _____ _____.

Gideon thought he was a nobody, but when he obeyed God, he discovered he was a "somebody"—a very important somebody.

Gideon was a winner. And you are, too, if you are on God's side.

Permission to photocopy this page granted for church use.

Permission to copy art granted for church use only.

Permission to copy art granted for church use only.

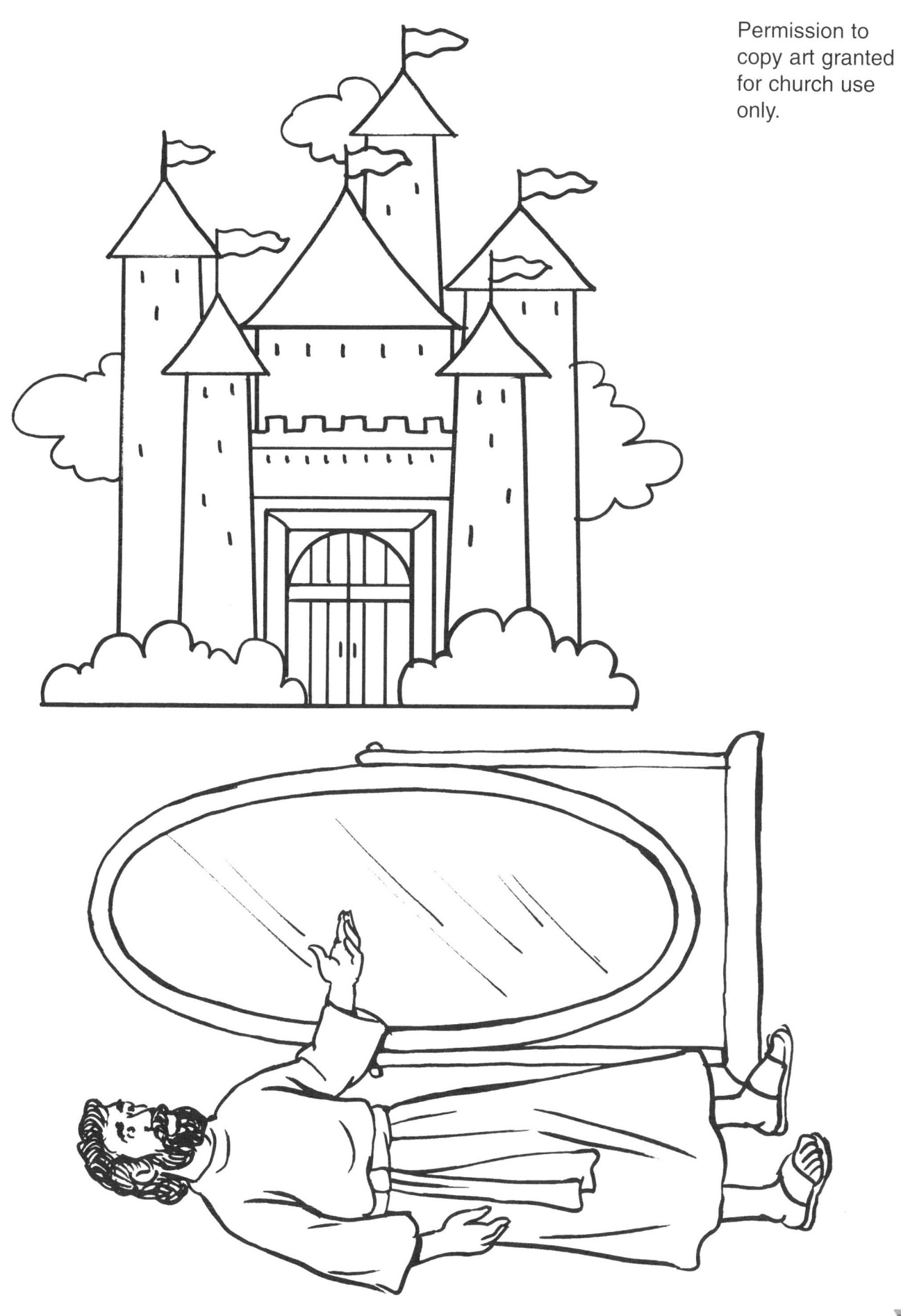

Permission to copy art granted for church use only.

Permission to copy art granted for church use only.

Carry the torch for MISSIONS

Every day
Give and Pray

Bring your offering to *kids POWer hour* for our special mission's project.

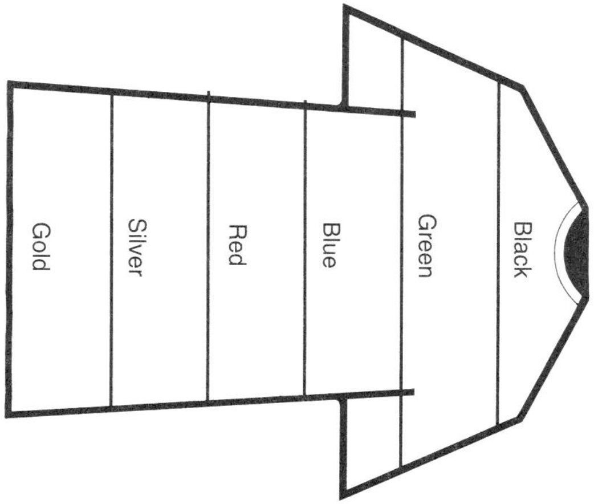

Place label around a can and glue or tape.

You are a winner!

1

Permission to copy art granted for church use only.

| Black |
| Green |
| Blue |
| Red |
| Silver |
| Gold |

Songs

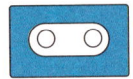

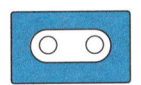

We Win!

(Sung by Tupelo Children's Mansion)

chorus:
We win! Hallelujah! we win!
I read the back of the book and
 we win!
We win! Hallelujah! we win!
I read the back of the book and
 we win!

Give and Pray

By Barbara Westberg

(Tune: "Send the Light")

Give and pray
That missionaries may go
Across the sea to preach the Word.
Give and pray
That missionaries may go
To share the love of the Lord.

Jesus Loves Even Me

I am so glad that Jesus loves me.
Jesus loves me, Jesus loves me.
I am so glad that Jesus loves me.
Jesus loves even me.

The Little Lamb

By Barbara Westberg

The little lamb loved to romp and play,
Until one day he went astray.
When the darkness fell all around,
The little lamb could not be found.

The shepherd left the sheep in the fold
And went looking in the cold,
For the little lamb that he loved so.
Where, oh where did his lamb go?

The shepherd looked all through
 the night.
He looked to the left and he looked to
 the right.
He found the lamb scared and cold,
And he brought him safely into
 the fold.

My Heart Was Black as Sin

My heart was black as sin
Until the Savior came in.
His precious blood I know
Has made me white as snow.
And in His Word I'm told
I'll walk on streets of gold.
Oh, wonderful, wonderful day!
He washed my sins away.

S-E-R-V-E

By Brenda Soptelean

(Tune: B-I-N-G-O)

There is a rule we must obey;
We'll serve Him every day.
S-E-R-V-E, S-E-R-V-E, S-E-R-V-E,
We'll serve Him every day.

There is a rule we must obey;
We'll serve Him when we pray.
S-E-R-V-E, S-E-R-V-E, S-E-R-V-E,
We'll serve Him when we pray.

There is a rule we must obey;
We'll read our Bible every day.
S-E-R-V-E, S-E-R-V-E, S-E-R-V-E,
We'll read our Bible every day.

Angels Watchin' Over Me

All night, all day,
Angels watchin' over me my Lord.
All night, all day,
Angels watchin' over me.

The Hebrew Boys

By Monette Moore

Daniel and the Hebrew boys would
 not eat the king's meat. No!
They did not eat. No!
They could not eat. No!
They would not eat. No!
They would not eat the king's meat.

Daniel and the Hebrew boys would
 not eat the king's meat. No!
It looked good. Uh-huh!
 (while rubbing stomach)
It smelled good. Yum! Yum!
 (pretend to sniff)
It probably tasted good.

Smack! Smack! (pretend to eat)
But they would not eat the king's meat.

Daniel and the Hebrew boys would
 not eat the king's meat. No!
Their skin was fairer,
 (look at hands)
They looked better,
 (hands around face)
They were stronger,
 (flex muscles)
Because they would not eat the
 king's meat.

Now there's a lesson to be learned
 from the Hebrew boys. Yes!
God will take care of you. Yes!
God will take care of you. Yes!
God will take care of you. Yes!
If you do what is right.

Mission Cheer

AIMER: **Missions, Missions is our theme.**
PUPPET/CHILDREN: **We're a mission-minded team.**
AIMER: **Missions, missions is our goal.**
PUPPET/CHILDREN: **Give to missions; win a soul.**
AIMER: **Can we do it?**
PUPPET: **Ab-so-lutely.**
CHILDREN: **Pos-i-tively.**
PUPPET: **Em-phat-ically.**
CHILDREN: **Un-mis-takably.**
PUPPET: **De-cid-edly—**
ALL: **Yes! M-I-S-S-I-O-N-S. Missions!**

PERMISSION TO
COPY GRANTED FOR
CHURCH USE ONLY.